God Without God

Writing with an admirable lucidity and following a tight line of argument, Michael Hampson outlines a credible Christian theology for the twenty-first century. Critical at times of both evangelical and catholic traditions, of both liberal and conservative thinking, he seeks to make faith accessible to those for whom established forms of belief have become inappropriate in the present-day context. **Canon David Peacock**, Former Pro-Rector, University of Surrey Roehampton

Western Christianity is at a major impasse, and this book gives you the major reasons why. As long as we have a punitive, petty God, whose love is entirely conditional, how can we expect history to be any different? Thank you, Michael Hampson! **Fr Richard Rohr OFM**, author of "Everything Belongs"

This is a moving account of a personal attempt to make sense of the Christian tradition in a rapidly changing social context. Hampson seeks to be faithful both to the biblical witness and Christian experience in order to help readers listen carefully to what the Spirit might be saying to the churches. **Revd Alan Le Grys**, Religion and Society, University of Kent

A heartfelt plea for a more humanistic approach to religious belief and practice. Hampson deserves credit for speaking out against the growing authoritarianism in church-governing circles, and both believers and atheists will profit from considering his thought-provoking arguments. **Stuart Sim**, Professor of Critical Theory, University of Sunderland, author of "Empires of Belief"

A challenging and inspiring enquiry into what may lie behind Western Christianity. "God without God" seeks to penetrate the mystery at the heart of faith and provides plenty of nourishment for theist and atheist alike. **Revd Canon Giles Goddard**, Chair of Inclusive Church

"God without God" is an ambitious book, and none the worse for that. It is well-written, in language that is generally non-technical but clear and accessible, and in an attractive style which is occasionally aphoristic... Strongly recommended. **Fr Brian O'Higgins**, RC Diocese of Brentwood

Michael Hampson has managed to articulate what many ordinary Christians in this country have long felt and believed, as they have sought to respond day by day to a loving God – in their everyday lives, and in their Christian communities. **Christopher Rowland**, Dean Ireland Professor of the Exegesis of Holy Scripture, Queen's College, Oxford

Michael Hampson addresses what has become the central religious challenge of our time for all those who regard themselves as the moderate majority: asserting a faith which is both rational and spiritually challenging, in tune with its historical and theological roots and yet able to address the circumstances of our own day. To that extent he has written his own Apologia, setting out a basis for faith grounded in an interpretation of scripture and the creeds and the sacramental life of the church.
This is a very personal account of faith, and a surprisingly conservative one. His confidence that this faith is relevant and necessary for human life and growth shines out of the book. For all those who are bewildered by the many currents of faith claiming to be the only possible one, whether liberal or conservative, and against a backdrop of assertive atheism, this is a very good guide through the essential elements of contemporary Christianity. An important and valuable contribution to the current religious debate. **Fr Simon Hobbs**, Grosvenor Chapel, London

Michael Hampson has written a compelling book, challenging Christians and atheists alike. He presents a deeply authentic spirituality which reaches into the profound mystery at the centre of Christian faith. He writes with feeling and intelligence, daring both conservative and liberal believers to move beyond projecting our human insecurities on to that mystery. Hampson offers an exciting read which encourages thinking people to rediscover a spirituality that connects the tradition with their experience. **Rt Revd Laurie Green**, Bishop of Bradwell

God Without God

Western Spirituality without the Wrathful King

Michael Hampson

BOOKS

Winchester, U.K.
New York, U.S.A.

First published by O Books, 2008
O Books is an imprint of John Hunt Publishing Ltd., The Bothy, Deershot Lodge, Park Lane, Ropley, Hants, SO24 0BE, UK
office1@o-books.net
www.o-books.net

Distribution in:

UK and Europe
Orca Book Services
orders@orcabookservices.co.uk
Tel: 01202 665432 Fax: 01202 666219 Int. code (44)

USA and Canada
NBN
custserv@nbnbooks.com
Tel: 1 800 462 6420 Fax: 1 800 338 4550

Australia and New Zealand
Brumby Books
sales@brumbybooks.com.au
Tel: 61 3 9761 5535 Fax: 61 3 9761 7095

Far East (offices in Singapore, Thailand, Hong Kong, Taiwan)
Pansing Distribution Pte Ltd
kemal@pansing.com
Tel: 65 6319 9939 Fax: 65 6462 5761

South Africa
Alternative Books
altbook@peterhyde.co.za
Tel: 021 447 5300 Fax: 021 447 1430

Text copyright Michael Hampson 2008

ISBN: 978 1 84694 102 3

All rights reserved. Except for brief quotations in critical articles or reviews, no part of this book may be reproduced in any manner without prior written permission from the publishers.

The rights of Michael Hampson as author have been asserted in accordance with the Copyright, Designs and Patents Act 1988.

A CIP catalogue record for this book is available from the British Library.

Printed in the US by Maple Vail

O Books operates a distinctive and ethical publishing philosophy in all areas of its business, from its global network of authors to production and worldwide distribution.

No trees were cut down to print this particular book. The paper is 100% recycled, with 50% of that being post-consumer. It's processed chlorine-free, and has no fibre from ancient or endangered forests. This production method on this print run saved approx. 13 trees, 4,000 gallons of water, 600 pounds of solid waste, 990 pounds of greenhouse gases and 8 million Btu of energy. On its publication a tree was planted in a new forest that O Books is sponsoring at The Village www.thefourgates.com

Contents

Introduction

The Christian faith stands accused of arrogance, hypocrisy, abuse of power, imperialism, dictatorship and genocide, discredited variously by science, rationalism, pluralism, Vatican politics and protestant fundamentalism, and finally rendered obsolete by democracy, wealth, technology, and even the church's own liberal wing. Once the monopoly player in the western spiritual marketplace, it looks increasingly like a bankrupt corporation destroyed by the weight of its own history.

God without God has no argument with science or atheism or pluralism - indeed it takes these as its premises, then sets out to explore what remains of the western spiritual tradition. It finds right at the heart of that tradition a concept of the divine far more complex and mysterious than that which the atheist rightly rejects. We move beyond theism and atheism to consider the mystery of existence itself, discovering a tradition full of contemporary resonance, with a profound and timeless integrity for body, mind and spirit.

Chapter 1
God

The case against God

As religion continues to dominate the national and international news, contemporary western society attempts to be both secular and pluralist: sympathetic to all religions but subservient to none.

These two ought to be incompatible. A more thoroughgoing secularism would be actively anti-religious, denouncing all religions alike for the harm they have done in the world. A more confident pluralism would be actively pro-religious, praising all religions together and promoting their united public role. With an intuitive wisdom, the contemporary social consensus takes the common theme from the two - that all religions are essentially the same - and reserves judgement on whether religion as a whole has done more harm than good, or more good than harm.

Behind the question of religion lies the more significant question of God. Contemporary society attempts to be equally diffident, but common ground between theism and atheism is more difficult to define.

A simplistic theism tends to maintain not only that God exists, but that God intervenes regularly in world affairs, from the global to the trivial, and has the right to demand obedience on threat of punishment. The greater presumption ahead of this detail is that there is only one such being, and that it has recognisable human attributes such as personhood and will. The whole package might be called not just theism but presumptive monotheism.

It is against this presumptive monotheism that the atheist case is made. The atheist argues that there is nothing in the observable universe that requires, or even suggests, the existence of such a God. Everything has been or will be explained by the sciences of physics, chemistry, biology, psychology, sociology and anthropology. The universe is a self-perpetuating, self-organising system: it needs no God to guide the planets in their courses, turn the acorn into an oak tree, open flowers in the meadow, or plan each human birth and death. It needs no God to make a parent love a child: that bond is a perfect example of the selfish gene looking after its own. Even altruism can evolve, as a population containing altruists is better equipped for survival than a population without. It was fashionable for a while to look for gaps in scientific explanations and place God there, but the gaps will diminish to nothing in time: a God in the gaps has no future. And there is a more emotive and assertive side to atheism: it refuses, as a matter of principle, to acknowledge a God who is all-powerful, yet allows unjust suffering, or who presumes to demand obedience on threat of punishment; even if such a God does exist, it has no right to our pathetic acquiescence.

The potential theist must come to terms with the truth of the atheist analysis. The wonders of the universe have all been explained, dependent on nothing but the big bang and a few simple constants; and there is no omnipotent God intervening to prevent human suffering or avenge every human injustice, at least not on the terms that we demand. Stripped of its mythology and metaphor, reduced to the bare historic facts of the case, the death by crucifixion of Jesus of Nazareth can serve as an icon for the absence of any interventionist God of justice. As we stand in the shadow of the cross, with the blood of the Nazarene dripping on the ground, God has forsaken the Christ, and forsaken us all.

The atheist case is sound, but is not the last word. The case is made against a very particular image of God, the God of presumptive monotheism, a God promoted by western kings and emperors in their own over-glorified self-image: autonomous, all-powerful, autocratic, wrathful, vengeful and demanding, with moments of random benevolence supposedly justifying the rest. For most of its history the papacy has been a secular power with all the same motivations for promoting the same false image of God, but theologians well away from the medieval Vatican, and all who live by faith, have a different understanding and experience of God, outside and beyond those images the atheist rightly rejects. Religion may have been used to justify wars, manipulate individuals, and crush the human spirit, but there remains a profound unity embracing the whole of humankind when the individual stands with open honesty before the mysteries of life and eternity.

God without God sets out to explore what happens to the western spiritual tradition when the God of presumptive monotheism - the wrathful king - is removed. Far from being destroyed or diminished, it flourishes in its liberation. It emerges from its captivity as an egalitarian, humanistic spirituality that challenges and defies all earthly powers in its celebration of the realm of the spirit, the realm of the divine.

Existence or Being

The church still claims two proofs for the existence of God, and they are entirely compatible with the atheist case against the God of presumptive monotheism. The first is the argument from creation: not that anything in the universe needs God in order to operate, but that anything exists at all, that there is even the space and the potential for anything to exist at all. It points to a mystery beyond the apes, the amoeba, the primeval soup, the complex carbons and the first expansion of the universe, to the ultimate source of all that exists and the essence of existence itself.[1]

The second begins with the experience of being self-consciously alive: the sense of being a conscious observer of, and decision-making participant in, the one particular life that we call our own. It points beyond measurable behaviour patterns, observable responses and evolutionary logic to the entirely personal experience of being self-consciously alive. As fragile and insignificant as it may seem against the vastness of the universe, the mystery of self-consciousness is the most significant experience in each of our lives, indeed the carrier of all our experience and the very essence of life. It points once again towards the mystery of existence itself.[2]

It is to this ultimate mystery that the church assigns first the name Existence or Being, 'which alone is without origin or end', and then the name God.[3] For now the word means only the ultimate mystery of existence itself: the two proofs tell us nothing of the nature of God, but they establish a concept to which we can assign the name, and in doing so, give us a place to begin. The argument has moved on from the existence or non-existence of God to the nature of the ultimate mystery of existence itself.

Yahweh Elohim

The Old Testament,[4] in the original Hebrew, has two names for God: Elohim/Eloah, and Yahweh. Elohim has the form of a masculine plural, Eloah has the form of a feminine singular. Both are translated into English as God. Elohim and Eloah emerge from a great melting pot of cultures and civilisations stretching from India to Ethiopia,[5] where many gods are honoured, both male and female. 'Hear, O Israel, the Lord your God is one Lord'[6] is not a pointless tautology, but the radical proclamation that all the gods are one. The continued use of Elohim/Eloah throughout the Old Testament acknowledges a reality that is complex and mysterious, unconstrained by gender, often appropriately plural, containing and embracing all goodness, all divinity, and ultimately all existence.

The one God who is Elohim/Eloah is given a more specific name, revealed to Moses at the burning bush.[7] It is derived from the verb to be, and is often rendered in translation as I Am. It could equally be 'the existing one', or the very concept of existence and reality itself, 'the ground of all being'. The name was regarded as too holy to be spoken. It is represented in the Hebrew text by four letters - the tetragrammaton - which would be passed over during recitation, or replaced with the Hebrew word Adoni, meaning Lord. This style is deliberately reproduced in the classic English translations, where the word is rendered in four capitals as LORD. We speak the word today as Jehovah or Yahweh (with a short 'a' and an aspirated middle 'h': Ya-hweh).[8]

These are ideal names for the mystery that lies at the heart of our existence: Elohim/Eloah, the sum of all divinity, with its structures both male and female, both singular and plural; and Yahweh, the ground of all being, to be used with such caution that it is barely to be spoken at all. The two names are used together - Yahweh Elohim - as naturally as Jesus and Christ. Together they encompass all that we hold sacred, and the fundamental concept of existence itself.

This dual name is carried forward into the original Greek of the New Testament.[9] Elohim/Eloah becomes Theos, translated as God: the context once again is a plurality of gods. For Yahweh/Adoni, the New Testament uses Kurios, translated as Lord. In general use, *kurios* can mean anything from the politeness of 'sir' to the absolute of 'master'. In the New Testament, and in the life of the early church, it resonates with meanings ranging from polite deference to the unspeakable majesty of the ground of all being.

In acknowledging God who is the ground of all being, we find ourselves in profound communion with the whole human race, for there is only one humankind, only one creation, and only one ground of all being. The Hindu faith recognises Brahman, the limitless one, ultimate being, beyond all the icons and incarnations. The Buddhist kneels in silence seeking to disconnect from the pain of this world and to connect instead with an essence or non-essence far more profound that lies beyond. The Sikh reaches out for the one God of all humankind, known in all authentic faiths, in meditation, worship and selfless service. The Buddhist seeks Buddha nature within each human soul, the Hindu faith speaks of *atman*, the presence of God in each individual, and our own tradition sees the image of God as the very essence of humankind.[10] All who seek to understand what it means to be human in the world, and who seek the potential for good in every human being, are reaching out for the same mystery. This includes those who assume the titles atheist or secular humanist to indicate their entirely proper rejection of many arbitrary and ultimately trivial images of God.

There is a group exercise, used on parish days away, where each person chooses a candle to represent them from a randomly mixed collection. Each explains their choice, and they begin to interact. They move around in a field of play representing the church or the world. God is sometimes added to the game as a wider and taller candle than all the rest combined – a typical image of God – but this candle gets in the way: nobody can relate to it, and it disrupts all the other interactions. If we remove that false image of God from the scene, a better image remains. God is not the biggest candle: God is the flame and the oxygen, the energy in the wax, the laws of physics making the whole thing possible, the potential in each one of us, the flame passed from one to the other, and the gentle breeze; the essence of existence itself, and the ultimate origin of everything; not the largest or the finest or the best, but literally beyond compare.

There was much intellectual sparring between atheist and Christian in the upper secondary and sixth form school years.[11] Eventually one long-time atheist found himself lying awake staring out of the window at the stars, half demanding and half pleading that God would send some tangible sign. He waited, and there was nothing: only the vast emptiness of space, and the silence. And he recognised God in the waiting, and in the emptiness, and in the silence.

God without God rejects the God of presumptive monotheism - the wrathful, autocratic, vengeful and demanding king - and acknowledges and seeks the God who is Yahweh Elohim, the ground of all being, and the essence of all that is good.

The Science of God

Western culture has come to imagine that science deals in facts. In reality, only a tiny proportion of science deals in facts, and these supposed facts are ultimately tautologies: the puzzles and games of pure mathematics, or theoretical physics, which work on the basis 'if this is true, this follows'. They are versions of philosophical logic: the 'if' defines their necessary disconnection from the real world.

The rest of science attempts to describe the real world

using a whole range of models and metaphors. Some of these models are robust and dependable, useful both inside the laboratory and out, providing working explanations for how things come to be as they are, and correctly predicting what will happen next. Others remain speculative and controversial, at the cutting edge of scientific investigation and debate. Scientific consensus is at its strongest where a single model or metaphor not only accounts consistently for a wide range of observations, but also connects seamlessly to models in use in other disciplines, as physics now connects to chemistry, and chemistry to biology. Beyond biology lie neurology, psychology and sociology, where rival models are in use and consensus is less common. At the opposite end of the scale, the cutting edge in physics also sees rival models in use. Light is described sometimes as a wave, and sometimes as a particle: in a camera, light behaves like a wave as it is focussed by the lens, and like a particle as it hits the film. This is science struggling with inadequate metaphors to describe a reality which is neither a wave nor a particle, but the unique mystery of light.

We are engaged in the same process when we attempt to speak of God: applying inadequate models and metaphors to describe a unique mystery.

Saint Thomas Aquinas (1225-1274), a key philosopher and theologian of the western tradition, has a profound respect for the mystery which is God. He asserts that God cannot be compared to any other thing, or placed in any category. To categorise is to define and limit according to concepts derived from the observable universe, and the mystery which is God lies beyond all these. It is limiting even to place God in the category of things that exist: if that category were to be defined in some way, and all the members of that category counted, giving a total of n, God is not the (n+1)th item in the category. In the same way God does not fit the category of beings, even the supposed category of spiritual beings; much less the categories of persons, kings, authorities, benefactors, or males. God is beyond all such earthly or human concepts, and yet, as the ground of all being, contains all the excellence, all the goodness, all the richness, of all these categories, and infinitely more besides. Existing things differ from God only in what they lack: God beyond compare contains it all. It follows that when we speak of God in metaphor, as king or lord or protector, or describe God in earthly attributes like powerful or merciful, we are always on the brink of diminishing God. And the moment we confuse the metaphor with the reality, we have created an idol, a false god in the image of created things.[12]

The Trinity

The idea of the Trinity is right at the heart of the western spiritual tradition, in popular devotion as much as academic theology; and yet it seems that every attempt at a detailed explanation of the model has been given a name, and declared to be a heresy. From the perspective of Saint Thomas Aquinas this makes perfect sense: God does not fit into categories of our making, including the category of triune beings. To invest too much in the theology of the Trinity is to confuse the reality with the metaphor. The question is not whether God exists as defined by some version of the doctrine of the Trinity, but whether the Trinity is a useful model by which to increase our understanding of the ultimate mystery which is God, our Yahweh Elohim. Addressing this possibility will mean examining the model in some detail.

Holy Spirit

Holy Spirit is the most accessible part of the model. Holy Spirit is God everywhere, inhabiting every corner of the universe, present in all that exists; and Holy Spirit is God active - or the emergence of a distinctive godliness - in particular people and places at particular times.

In the bible, spirit is *ruach* in Hebrew and *pneuma* in Greek, both of which mean breath or wind. In the sense of breath, spirit is the essence of life: the spirit of God is the very essence of the life of God. The sense of spirit as wind is captured in the words of Jesus: 'The *pneuma* blows where it wills, and you hear the sound of it, but you cannot tell where it comes from or where it is going; so it is with everyone who is born of the *pneuma*'.[13] Those who have tried to define or even control the action of the *pneuma* have been chasing after the wind: the spirit blows where it wills, and will not be captured in our categories.

Abba pater

Jesus invites us to think of Yahweh Elohim as father. He uses the word *abba,* the equivalent of our *dada,* which is the trusting murmur of the infant to the father; also *pater,* which is not only origin and source but also nourisher, protector and upholder. Jesus encourages us to rejoice in the simple goodness of the world around us, let go of our anxieties, and trust in the ultimate goodness of our *abba pater* God. 'Look at the birds of the air: they neither sow nor reap, nor gather into barns, but your heavenly father feeds them'.[14]

The fullest explanation of the image is given in the parable of the prodigal son:[15] Jesus describes a father who grants us our full inheritance right now, and the freedom to do with it as we please. When we waste it all and return home in desperation we find not the expected condemnation but only more grace.[16] Day after day the father has been standing at the door watching for our return. When he sees our sad figure on the horizon he gathers up his robes and runs to welcome us home with an embrace. Indifferent to the prepared apology, he declares a feast. This is not the wrathful, vengeful and demanding God of presumptive monotheism: this is the God who nourishes us, holds us close, lets us go, and welcomes us home without condition. Neither is it an image constrained by conventional models of fatherhood: middle-eastern fathers do not submit to the indignity of running in their robes; and for good measure, at least once in the New Testament, *pater* is used in the plural to mean parents without regard to gender.[17] The parable continues with the sad story of the elder son who never left home, and who resents the generous treatment of the returning prodigal: this is Jesus's commentary on the sad state of those who have laboured bitterly at their religion for many years, failing to recognise the compassion and generosity of their *abba pater* God.[18]

Eventually Jesus invites us to address Yahweh Elohim directly as 'our father in the heavens'.[19] The heavens here are *ouranois*, a plural form of *ouranos*, which in common use means the sky, as in 'the sky is red',[20] or the air, as in 'the birds of the air'.[21] It shares its origin with words meaning covering and encompassing. Jesus's father *en ouranois* is our father all around us, in the sky and in the air we breathe, inhabiting, encompassing, covering and embracing all creation. These are images entirely in keeping with our established concept of Yahweh Elohim as the ground of all being and the sum of all divinity. The question remaining is whether Yahweh Elohim is indeed *abba pater:* not only our ultimate origin and source, but also nourisher, protector and upholder, and even the bearer of limitless compassion, as the parable of the prodigal implies.[22]

With Yahweh Elohim understood as the ground of all

being, our assessment of Yahweh Elohim's benevolence, malevolence or indifference will depend as much on our assessment of the fundamental nature of the world around us as on any theory about God. Insofar as any of us has made it from conception to adulthood, the world around us has indeed been, in the most literal sense, our nourisher, protector and upholder; and it has been argued that the world as we know it is the best of all possible worlds: that any alteration in the balance of pleasure and pain would result in a worse situation, not a better one; that the suffering now present in the world is the minimum possible given the existence of human free will. The opposite argument can also be made: that this is the worst of all possible worlds; that there is just enough pleasure in the world to highlight the wretchedness of the rest of our existence. To counter both arguments, it has also been suggested that we would experience the same balance of pleasure and pain whatever our situation: we all know people who remain content whatever their circumstances, and others who likewise remain miserable regardless, and we learn that on an average day we can choose to be one or the other. In the end we have no way of knowing whether this is the best or the worst of all possible worlds, or anything in between. What we can do is choose how to see it, and how to live in it: we choose a working model or metaphor by which to make sense of, and then interact with, realities we cannot fully know.

There is a working model or metaphor for understanding human life that casts love or compassion as the central principle. It argues that love, in all its diversity, is what people seek; and that finding it, they find their fulfilment. Like the best of scientific metaphors it links together many disciplines: it describes countless beneficial human relationships, and accounts for many negative experiences as well, where these are caused by dysfunctional or failed attempts to find the attention, affection, acceptance and companionship that otherwise belong with human compassion.

The model is built on experience and observation - it requires no divine intervention or revelation - and yet, almost accidentally, it defines the nature of Yahweh Elohim: it declares compassion to be the central principle of life - the fundamental essence of being - which we have been calling Yahweh; and in declaring compassion to be our ultimate fulfilment, it makes compassion our goal and ideal, and effectively our God, which is Elohim/Eloah, the sum of all divinity. If we adopt this model, God is indeed *abba pater:* Yahweh Elohim becomes by definition the origin and sum, the beginning and end, the essence and purpose, of all love and compassion.

The model is resonant with echoes from scripture. Jesus summarises the entire message of the Old Testament - both the law and the prophets - as 'Love God and love your neighbour'.[23] Saint Paul insists that no quantity of good works or spiritual gifts is worth anything without love.[24] Saint John asserts directly that God is love.[25] This quotation from Saint John introduces the first encyclical of Pope Benedict XVI, published in 2005, a fifteen-thousand word meditation on the wonder of love in all its aspects, and on its place at the very heart of the western spiritual tradition.[26]

It could be argued instead that the default assumption should be not benevolence but indifference from Yahweh Elohim and the universe. This model is not as negative as it may sound, indeed it can be something of a liberation. If Yahweh Elohim is indifferent to our welfare, then we live as we choose, and neither God nor the universe shows any interest. There is no punishment ahead, and no judgement, and life is what we make it. It makes each of us an adult, not a servant or a child. We are free to make our own choices and build our own lives.

Beginning with this model, whether by deliberate

choice or by default, many have found, with experience and perspective, that love is the key to living well. In recognising love or compassion as the foundation of life, and making it their goal and ideal, these also live with love or compassion as both Yahweh and Elohim.

Many will contend however that defining the nature of Yahweh Elohim as love or compassion takes insufficient account of the suffering in the world, and propose that there has to be a malevolent streak within our model of God, often expressed as a divine obligation to punish wrongdoing. Such an obligation represents the return of the wrathful king, passing judgement and dealing punishment.

Others propose, instead or in addition, a malevolence existing not within God, but as the enemy of God. The biblical *satanas* can be any challenge or challenger - it often represents the unwelcome voice of temptation or accusation[27] - and we all have our demons: they torment us, tear us apart, and damage our lives and relationships. Mostly they are demons of our own making: secrets, lies and hidden pain. These can be useful metaphors, but to grant them independent existence - even personhood - is to push them too far. We are cautious of strong metaphors even for God: much more so for the supposed enemies of God. Too many religious people have turned the devil and his demons into idols, and even into gods, with whom they are obsessed, and whom they actively pursue. Malevolence, hatred, suffering and pain are real, and we can speak of them, but in ascribing underlying causes we are using metaphors, which should not become confused with the often much simpler reality. More importantly, we have been understanding Yahweh Elohim as the ground of all being and the ultimate source of all that exists, beyond all human categories: the ground of all being can have no external rival or enemy without having an internal malevolence as well.

A biblical metaphor for malevolence and suffering is the contrast between darkness and light.[28] Darkness is a tangible reality with tangible effects, yet in literal terms it does not exist in its own right at all: it is only the absence of light. By analogy we can acknowledge malevolence and suffering as tangible realities, yet define their existence not as the presence of evil but as the absence of good. This aligns with Aquinas's notion that existing things differ from God only in what they lack. Again, too many religious people live as though the opposite were true: as though goodness did not exist in its own right, but only as the absence of evil, so that anything touched by any hint of impurity itself becomes tainted and irreparably impure; this model casts the devil and his works as strong, and God and goodness as powerless against them; it is a dangerously false model, with its advocates prone to judgementalism and a false self-righteousness in the face of their own impossible quest for purity. In the biblical model, when light meets darkness, there is only light.

The remaining mystery is how there can be any darkness at all with a God of light. Much human suffering has its origin in human free will: we bring it on ourselves through our own choices, and we inflict it on each other. Even a so-called natural disaster is the interaction of an otherwise benign natural phenomenon with a particular human choice, such as living on the side of a volcano. And the free will concept can be extended to the volcano, the lightening strike and the movement of the oceans, each of them phenomenally beautiful were it not for the human populations affected: there is a sense in which every particle of creation, or even creation as a whole, might be said to have free will - the free will that produces the beauty of the night sky, the mountains and the valleys, the whole realm of biodiversity and ultimately the human race itself. There is an image in the

Jewish tradition, relating to the moment of creation, that sees God moving sideways, or creating a space within God, to make room for the universe to exist: surrendering omnipotence, to allow free will. It would be a major inhibition of free will if God were to intervene to prevent every negative consequence of every human choice, and human life without the experience of free will would be unimaginably trivial. We end up with shadows, where the light is less intense, as part of the deal whereby Yahweh Elohim, the God of light, our benevolent *abba pater*, allows creation free will.

Of the three major aspects of the Trinity, *abba pater* is the most neglected and abused. The Father is routinely represented as an authoritarian, disciplinarian figure, entirely at odds with the images used by Jesus himself. This is the wrathful king forced into the role of dysfunctional parent. In that role, he inevitably becomes the dominant aspect of the Trinity, with Jesus and the Spirit demoted to mere helpers or hangers on. This demotion is recognised as heresy - the authentic western tradition insists that all three are equally God - but creeps through nevertheless into countless formal prayers, which are routinely addressed to God, 'through Jesus Christ our Lord, who lives and reigns with you and the Holy Spirit', not only creating a heretical Trinity of God, Jesus and the Holy Spirit, but overlooking the essential and radical teaching of Jesus on the fatherhood of God.

Serving in the role of dysfunction parent, the wrathful king has been keen to preserve his self-image as a powerful male warrior. The concept of mother earth has been regarded as an enemy of this image of God, the goddess of a false religion opposed to all that the wrathful king represents. With God understood not as the wrathful king, but as Yahweh the ground of all being, and as Elohim/Eloah - both male and female, both singular and plural, the sum of all divinity - the imagery associated with the mother earth metaphor is welcome in the pantheon of metaphors which is both Yahweh and Elohim, and fits most naturally within the Trinity as part of the imagery of the nurturing, protecting and upholding ultimate source.

God beyond the metaphors remains unconstrained by any human category, including the categories of male and female, but for the record, the Old Testament Hebrew word for Spirit - *ruach* - is a feminine noun, and the Greek New Testament equivalent, *pneuma,* is neuter. We have already seen that *pater* can be used without regard for gender; and Elohim/Eloah is the all-embracing ungendered plural in the ground of all being, Yahweh Elohim, our God of infinite compassion.

The Christ

It is the concept of the Christ that most explicitly joins God to humankind.

The key to making sense of the concept of God in human form lies neither in Nazareth nor in Bethlehem, but in Genesis, in the story of creation. God (as Elohim) declares, 'Let us make humankind in our image, and after our likeness', and immediately creates humankind 'in the very image of Elohim'.[29] We are called to recognise and acknowledge the image of God in all humankind - an original, fundamental godliness - no matter how much it has been marred, neglected, damaged or obscured by the years. We are also alerted to the intriguing possibility that a perfect human being would be a perfect image of God, both fully human and fully divine.

This imagined being - both fully human and fully divine - is our definition of the Christ of faith. It is a powerful addition to the Trinity. It draws into our concept of Yahweh not only the essence of all being but the essence specifically of what it is to be human; and it draws into our concept of Elohim all the richness of the full diversity of humankind. It completes a trinity of images or metaphors for God in which Yahweh Elohim is *ruach* and *pneuma* (the breath and the wind), *abba pater en ouranois* (the universal nourisher, protector and upholder), and finally, in the Christ of faith, the perfect union of the human and the divine.

The inclusion of the Christ of faith in the Trinity makes for a profoundly egalitarian and humanistic spirituality. If all humankind alike is made in the image of God, there is no blue blood of royalty, nor any chosen caste or race, and all stand equal before God. Saint Paul affirms that in Christ there is neither Jew nor Greek, male nor female, slave nor free;[30] and to put the arrogant in their place, asserts that all alike have sinned and fallen short of the glory of God,[31] making all equally dependent on the grace of God. Those who receive that grace Saint Paul routinely describes as 'in Christ' (*en Christo*), and the Christian community as a whole as 'the body of Christ' (*soma Christou*), drawing redeemed humankind right into the godhead. The gospels challenge us to recognise and serve Christ not only in one another within the Christian community but in the needy around us as well,[32] and the Christian community declares the Christ to be truly present in its symbolic meal of bread and wine.[33]

With God made tangibly, physically present in the community of faith, in other people, and in the meal of bread and wine, our Trinity could now appear complete, not as any dogmatic claim about a reality out there, but as a profound meditation on our existence, our hopes, and our highest ideals, understood first as Yahweh Elohim, the ground of all being and the sum of all divinity, and then as *abba* and *ruach* and the Christ of faith, with no order of pre-eminence amongst the three, each carrying equal weight as part of this working model or metaphor for existence itself – but the western tradition has one final element to add to the mix. It goes on to identify one specific, historic human being with the Christ of faith, namely Jesus of Nazareth. The contemporary church is sympathetic, indeed generous, in its assessment of other world faiths and belief systems, but holds up this link with Jesus of Nazareth as the essential factor that defines the Christian faith, and therefore the authentic western spiritual tradition.[34]

It is not unreasonable to choose to affirm that the historic Jesus of Nazareth is one with the Christ of faith. It all depends on our image of Yahweh Elohim so far. We are not imagining Yahweh Elohim as a distant presumptuous Superior Being for whom appearance in human form would be a scandalous anomaly: rather we have understood Yahweh Elohim as close to creation, embracing and upholding it all, containing all the excellence of everything that exists. We see this divinity breaking through in every beautiful and wholesome aspect of creation, in every human individual, and in every act of compassion. We can all acknowledge individuals who have shown in their lives the best of what it is to be human, and who have therefore shown glimpses of the divine, whether a parent, a friend, a teacher, a Ghandi or a Mandela. The first invitation is to rank our inspirations, placing Jesus of Nazareth in first rank. The second is to name that individual not only our inspiration and example, but our chosen ideal, our leader and guide, and even our God. These were the choices of the first disciples and the early Christian communities. They are the choices of the Christian community today.

Choosing to believe that a particular individual in history is one with the Christ of faith adds significantly to our model or metaphor for Yahweh Elohim. It affirms with absolute clarity that our divinely valued humanity includes not just our thought life, but our physical life as well.

Greek philosophy at the time of the early church valued our thought life and despised our physical life, to the extent that the word *pneuma* (wind/breath/spirit) was used to mean everything good about humankind, and the word *sarx* (meat/flesh) to mean everything bad. Saint Paul follows the same convention, using *pneuma* to mean all that is good in human motivations and behaviours, and *sarx* to mean all that is bad: he then uses *soma* (body) for both the body of Christ and the human body, and is content for the human *soma* (in contrast to *sarx*) to be redeemed,[35] holy and acceptable to God,[36] a member of Christ,[37] and a temple of the Holy Spirit in which God can be glorified.[38]

Saint John addresses the Greek denial of the body more directly: he identifies the eternal Christ with the venerated Greek concept of *Logos* or the eternal Word, which is logic, rationality and wisdom, then states clearly, in words deliberately designed to scandalise, that the Word became flesh (*ho logos sarx egeneto*)[39] in Jesus of Nazareth.

With a specific human individual identified as the Christ of faith, our entire ordinary humanity - including our mammalian fleshiness - is drawn into the realm of the divine. Our eating and drinking, our walking and dancing, our health and fitness, our home-making and our love-making, our very flesh and bones, are all affirmed as expressions of the image of God in which we are made. It is the concept known as the incarnation, the enfleshment, of God: God truly present in ordinary matter, in the practical physical material of daily life.

In placing the imagined Christ of faith in the Trinity first, and identifying the concept with Jesus of Nazareth second, we have used the benefit of historic perspective to approach these questions in reverse. Historically, Jesus of Nazareth does not request admission to a pre-existing Trinity: rather the entire Trinitarian model is built around him, as the first disciples and then the early church seek to understand their unique experience of God in Jesus Christ.

In the earliest preserved writings of the Christian community - the New Testament scriptures - this understanding has reached a stage where the historic Jesus is acknowledged as God or Son of God.[40] In the following decades and centuries, the great councils of the church, in handling this potential paradox, tread a careful path between models that deny Jesus's full humanity and those which deny his full divinity, eventually defining Jesus as both fully human and fully divine. The Trinitarian model evolves in parallel. The eastern tradition tends to emphasise the relationship between the Father and the Son, and in one version characterises the Holy Spirit not as a third person in that relationship but as the relationship itself, and the love overflowing from it.[41] In the western tradition, Father, Son and Holy Spirit are three persons equal in one Godhead.

The model complete

Staring at the western model for too long tends to result in the appearance of three gods, which is either arbitrarily few or two too many, often with Jesus in particular looking like the odd one out, having a human side as well as a divine side. I used to prefer to tell a story: that God the creator did not leave us to it, but walked amongst us in Jesus the Christ, and is with us now as Holy Spirit. Later I preferred a story with Jesus of Nazareth at the centre: that he reveals the Father, and sends us the Spirit.

Others have found a richness in contemplating not so much the three persons of the Trinity as the nature of the relationships between them, making those relationships themselves the essential nature of God: they speak of the love of God beginning within God, within the Trinity, or more poetically speak of the community of the Trinity or even the dance of the Trinity being the essential nature of God. We already have a name for such a model, and it is Elohim.

Now I prefer to remember that the Trinity is only a working model or metaphor for the complex mystery which is God, who is the ground of all being and the sum of all divinity, and who fits none of our earthly categories. It is a model that gives a place to our chosen leader and guide, our example and our God, Jesus of Nazareth, while enriching our concept of Yahweh Elohim by bringing it even closer to our ordinary earthly humanity.

I have written elsewhere of how both the bible and the western tradition in practice allow a fluidity in their imagery for God, with the three aspects of the Trinity merging into each other to re-emerge variously as omnipotent God, creator, Father, eternal Word, Jesus of Nazareth, the Risen Christ, the Spirit of Christ, Holy Spirit, omnipresent God, and even the Great Creator Spirit of Eastern Orthodox prayer, all of these being aspects of the one God who is *ruach, abba* and Christ.[42] The Trinity is a flexible working model or metaphor for God. It is the current state of the science of God.

God without God

We begin with the affirmation of the atheist case against the God of presumptive monotheism. We move on to the affirmation of a mystery: the mystery of the existence of the world around us and of our own self-consciousness within in. For that mystery we take the Old Testament name for God: Yahweh Elohim, the ground of all being and the sum of all divinity, surrounding, indwelling and embracing all that exists. Then in the western tradition we name infinite compassion as our God - our Yahweh Elohim - and Jesus of Nazareth as its incarnation.

We could have made the entire journey from the outset in reverse order, beginning with Jesus of Nazareth. Searching for ideals by which to live, and a model by which to understand all the joy and sorrow of the human condition, we hold up the icon of this dying human being and say: this is our inspiration, our leader, our God. We subvert this very human symbol of worldly oppression and failure and make it the banner of our radical humanistic faith. We tell his story amongst ourselves once again, and share bread and wine in his name. We declare the infinite compassion to which he calls us to be our God also, and declare that his spirit is amongst us, and we have our trinity once again.

In choosing to name infinite compassion as our God, and in naming Jesus of Nazareth its incarnation, we make choices that atheism cannot take away; and far from being dependent upon it, this authentic Trinity does not even have room for the arbitrary, wrathful and condemning God of presumptive monotheism. We are beyond theism and atheism, making practical choices about how to live our lives, with Christ crucified - representing infinite compassion - as the ideal and icon of our faith and spirituality. We use the much-abused word God as little as possible, only ever with caution, always pausing to reflect: it means existence, being, ultimate reality and mystery, and infinite compassion; it means Jesus of Nazareth, and the sum of all ideals, and the essence of life itself. It must never mean any of those presumptions that the atheist rightly rejects.

We might ask again in what sense this God exists, beyond our model and metaphor, beyond theism and atheism. Certainly there is compassion, identifiable and existing, in the world, perhaps even in every human heart, variously as reality, longing and goal. If nothing else, we can assert that the sum total of this identifiable compassion does exist, and we can name that sum total as our existent God. Even if no compassion remained in the world we could name the concept and the potential as our God, and it would exist as concept and potential. More fundamentally, if anything exists at all, Yahweh exists by definition as the ground of all being; and if anything is considered wonderful and good, or colloquially 'divine', then Elohim exists by definition as the sum of all divinity.

Perhaps the question might be rephrased, to consider whether this compassionate essence, our Yahweh Elohim, not only exists, but has personhood and will. Mindful that God does not fit any of our categories, including personhood, and that we must not confuse the metaphor with the far greater reality beyond, nevertheless we might allow personhood a place in our metaphor, on the basis that the sum total of all compassion demands personhood because of the nature of compassion, in a way that the sum total of all colour or the sum total of all sound does not. Having granted personhood, we might also grant will: not the arbitrary will of presumptive monotheism and its autocratic, opinionated and wrathful king, but the perfect will of infinite compassion.

We are beyond theism and atheism and into the reality of Yahweh Elohim, known to us as *abba pater en ouranois* (our sustainer in the skies), and Jesus of Nazareth, and *ruach,* the spirit or breath of God.

It is possible that our metaphor has already become too strong. At least being founded on compassion it has not become harmful or dangerous, like so much of religion: it is entirely life-enhancing and life-enriching. There is nothing to fear in the possibility that there is no God beyond the skies, that life ends at death, that this life is all there is, with no meaning beyond itself; that the future is non-existence, without retribution, reward or recompense. In the contemplation of this final rest we may even find contentment and peace. The greater fear is that our metaphor is too weak: that there is, after all, an arbitrary God of wrath and condemnation; but if there is such a God, we are lost already, condemned either to his wrath or to a desperate, pathetic servitude. If God is not a God of love, there is no hope, and no point in believing.

We began by rejecting the God of presumptive monotheism - the wrathful, autocratic, vengeful and demanding king - and seeking instead Yahweh Elohim, the ground of all being and the essence of all that is good. We are exploring what happens to the western spiritual tradition when the God of presumptive monotheism is removed. So far we find that its Trinity is intact: a valuable metaphor for understanding the mystery of Yahweh Elohim as *pater, ruach,* and fully human incarnation; as infinite compassion, that blows where it wills, and finds expression in human form.

Introducing the mass

The concept of the incarnation affirms that God is truly present in ordinary matter, in the practical physical material of daily life; in the beggar on the street and in anyone who stops to help; in the battered wife, and in the women who run the hostel that takes her in; in the neon lights of a busy street; in the bread and wine of a simple meal. It ties together all our metaphors for God and brings them home. It brings us back to the simplicity of Yahweh Elohim, who is existence itself, and the sum of all ideals.

While God is present in all human beings, in all living things, and in all creation, the church has traditionally invited us to focus on particular materials, particular actions, particular moments and particular ceremonies to remind us of this universal truth. These are the sacraments, each one a reminder of the principle of the incarnation: God present in the practical, physical stuff of ordinary life. Popular catholic culture happily extends the sacramental principle to include candles, incense, bells, processions, statues, paintings, church decoration, palms on Palm Sunday, ashes on Ash Wednesday, medallions of the saints and rosaries for Mary. The number of official sacraments has varied over the centuries but stands today at seven. The sacraments are the ongoing incarnation: the presence and work of God made tangible in the contemporary world.

Supreme amongst the seven is the meal of bread and wine: holy communion, the eucharist, the mass. The people gather around the scriptures and the sacrament, then go out into the world to the live the life. To continue our exploration of the western tradition, we go now to mass, for the mass holds every aspect of the tradition in its embrace. In the following chapters we shall hear the key words of the mass, and follow its form, as we explore the western tradition with our new perspective. Within this context we shall encounter all but one of the remaining contemporary sacraments - reconciliation, anointing for healing, baptism, confirmation and holy order - leaving only the seventh sacrament, holy matrimony, with its own distinct and universal nature, for consideration outside the mass. Within the tradition, each of the seven sacraments is an incarnation of the real presence of Yahweh Elohim, the ground of all being and the sum of all that is good.

This may all sound very catholic in a protestant-dominated world, but this is the authentic western tradition. Protestantism and atheism both rightly emerge in the west in protest against the image of God as a wrathful medieval king. Atheism ends up preserving and nurturing that image in order to keep on rejecting it, setting up an entirely false argument against people of faith, into which people of faith have allowed themselves to be drawn, defending an image of God they might otherwise easily reject. Protestantism also ends up preserving the same false image of God, with an ever more complex theology surrounding it, explaining how the wrathful king might have his wrath appeased by the death of his own son. If we drop that monolithic image of a wrathful king, we can move beyond theism and atheism into the realities of Yahweh Elohim, the trinity, and the authentic western tradition.

Today there are more than a billion Roman Catholics in the world, and the number continues to grow.[43] All forms of protestantism combined number less than half that figure, and almost a third of those are represented by the two largest protestant denominations, Lutheranism and Anglicanism, which are historically the most catholic of protestants; the rest are divided by a thousand schisms.[44] The Roman Catholic church began its own reformation-era reforms at the Council of Trent in 1545, but remained compromised by the corrupting influence of direct earthly power. It finally conceded the loss of the last of the papal lands in 1929, and by 1962 was ready for its most significant internal reforms since the reformation era, at the Second Vatican Council, where it once again laid confident claim to the authentic western spiritual tradition.[45]

As we gather for the mass, we leave aside the ambiguous word God, and gather instead in this threefold name. These are the first words we hear: 'In the name of the Father, and of the Son, and of the Holy Spirit. Amen.'

And then we bring the three together in the ancient word *kurios*, with its resonances ranging from public good manners to Yahweh, the ground of all being, and a direct link to the first Christian creed, the playfully ambiguous 'Jesus is *kurios*', Jesus is Lord. The ancient Christian greeting, at the opening of the mass to this day, is 'The Lord be with you'.

Chapter 2
Ethics

From Eden to the Cross

The concept of sin has taken a prominent place in every version of western religion: it has become fundamental to the western image of God. We need to determine what role this concept might have when the wrathful, autocratic, vengeful and demanding God is rejected in favour of a ground of all being and sum of all divinity whose nature is infinite compassion. At its worst, the western understanding of sin has been about arbitrary law, the demand for obedience, and the infliction of punishment. At its best, it has been about understanding, then reducing, and finally healing, the harm that we inflict on ourselves and one another.

The punitive model retains its power amongst so many of the faithful by bringing together two powerful biblical images: Eden and the cross. Every Sunday School child knows the Eden story - God tells the first human couple not to eat from one particular tree, they eat from it anyway, and God evicts them from the garden as punishment for their wilful disobedience - but Genesis was not written as a story book for children, and if we return to the text, we find a far more complex account. There are two trees involved. The only tree from which Adam and Eve are not to eat is called the tree of the knowledge of good and evil. Eating that fruit, and acquiring that knowledge, they find themselves overwhelmed by shame. To protect them from further foolishness God removes them from the garden lest they eat also from the tree of life, which would condemn them to live for ever in their fallen state. There is neither arbitrary law nor punishment here, but a complex myth shedding far more light on our imperfect and mortal state than the usual superficial reading allows.[1]

The punitive interpretation of the Eden episode is extended to the cross. This central icon of the Christian faith is presented as the final punishment for sin: Jesus voluntarily takes upon himself the punishment that we deserve, winning forgiveness for the faithful. This model presents a God who appears to have no choice but to exact punishment for all wrongdoing, who bizarrely accepts third-party payment, and who finally has his wrath assuaged by the death of his own son. As an image of God it could hardly be further removed from the images presented by Jesus himself. It was an image popular with medieval kings and emperors, allowing them to claim divine mandate for their own arbitrary systems of law, wrath and condemnation. It remains popular amongst religious leaders today for many of the same reasons - but the faithful know intuitively that it must be wrong. They experience a God of grace, not a God of wrath and law.

With Saint Paul, the faithful understand that sin is not primarily an argument with God, but a battle within ourselves, and a concept and experience far more complex than any list of prohibited actions. They see Jesus delighting in ordinary human virtues, not counting and condemning every human weakness. They hear him denouncing the self-righteousness and hypocrisy of those who boast of their religious purity. They see him undermining the legalistic model by declaring forgiveness recklessly, without first discussing conditions like repentance or recompense. They hear Saint Paul railing against the curse of legalism, and struggling to describe the higher virtue of the life of faith lived in the grace of God.

The faithful tend to resolve that God is not only forgiving, but generously so; and yet the idea that God has to choose to forgive at all suggests lingering traces of wrath and condemnation. We learn by our own experience that anger and unforgiveness can destroy the soul: that they are human failings, not attributes of the divine. It would be more accurate to say not that God is generously forgiving, but that in God there can be no trace of unforgiveness. God longs only to restore us from the damage we inflict on ourselves and one another.

Part of the attraction of the punitive model is that it gives the crucifixion a great cosmic purpose, but the true horror of the cross is that it has no purpose. It is a pointless slaughter, humankind murdering another of its own. The religious and political leaders conspired to bring it about - as is so often the case throughout history - but there is a part of every one of us that was there in spirit: denying him, betraying him, holding the nails, hammering them in. It did not require some great cosmic deal to put Jesus on the cross: just ordinary human beings doing what we ordinarily do. Far from magically solving the complex problem of sin, it merely kills another innocent human being, and proves once again that there is no justice in the world. It rightly becomes the iconic moment representing all the sin of humankind.

The episode only makes sense when considered as a whole, from the nativity to the ascension.[2] It is sometimes implied that the only purpose of the life was the death. On the contrary, the only purpose of the death was the living of a fully human life. God lived that fully human life in Christ because it is in the very nature of God to do so. Suffering at our hands was the inevitable consequence, and was not counted sufficient reason to stay away. The cross rightly becomes the iconic moment representing all the grace of God. That grace alone is the solution to the problem of sin.

Meditations and metaphors around the events of Good Friday validly draw in many themes as we try to comprehend the horror of what we did and why God allowed it to happen, but metaphors pushed too far can obscure a much simpler truth. The suffering of the incarnate life was the price God paid to be the forgiving and generous God that we know - to be true to the nature of God - but nobody received the payment. It was a ransom in the sense that our rescue was costly, but no captor received the fee. It was a sacrifice in the sense that those with high ideals make sacrifices for the sake of a higher goal, but not in the sense that there was a vengeful deity's wrath to be appeased by receiving the sacrifice. The blood of Jesus wins our salvation in the sense of life-blood: in our culture, blood has become a symbol of death instead of life; life-blood is the one English usage that accurately captures the biblical sense. All these images go wrong when the metaphor takes over or becomes corrupted in translation: when the ransom demands a captor, or the sacrifice demands a wrathful and unforgiving God, or blood begins to symbolise death instead of life. But meditations and metaphors can still be helpful, so here is one more: there is nothing worse the human race can do than crucify the son of God; as we commit this worst of all possible offences, he says, 'Father forgive'; our salvation is won on the cross, as in those words the compassion of God overcomes all evil.

Damage to the heart: mortal and venial

In the Church of England's 1980 Baptism Service, two of the questions to parents and godparents are 'do you repent of your sins' and 'do you renounce evil'.[3] I used to say the first question referred to all the things we do every day and know that we shouldn't, and the second to the half dozen moments in our lives when we are faced with the real possibility of doing something major for our own satisfaction that we know to be utterly wrong. The first response - 'I repent of my sins' - is a promise to be the best we can be day by day; the second - 'I renounce evil' - is a pledge for the sake of the child and all humankind that when those moments of temptation come, we will make the right choice.

There is no clear boundary between sin and evil, but we know there is a contrast here. In the catholic tradition it is the difference between mortal and venial sin. These become essential concepts in understanding sin not as an offence against an arbitrary and wrathful God, but as damage that we inflict upon ourselves. Committing venial sin offends and wounds the compassion of the heart; committing mortal sin destroys it.[4]

In practical terms, for sin to be defined as mortal, three conditions apply. It must be a *grave matter*, and it must executed with both *full knowledge* and *complete consent*. The definition of grave matter is not precise, but the ten commandments are suggested as a starting point: a top ten list of serious issues. Full knowledge means the action is known to be unambiguously wrong, and complete consent means the action is deliberately chosen, after full consideration and without duress. If any of these three conditions is not met, the matter is venial rather than mortal: the compassion of the heart is offended and wounded, but not destroyed.[5]

The damage done to the heart begins to heal - and the relationship with God is restored - the very moment there is *perfect contrition*. This is defined as 'a sorrow of the soul and detestation for the sin committed, together with the resolution not to sin again', all arising from 'a love by which God is loved above all else'.[6] Inevitably such perfect contrition will be accompanied by a desire to 'do what is possible in order to repair the harm (return stolen goods, restore the reputation of someone slandered, pay compensation for injuries)', and by a desire to cooperate with God in the healing of the sinner's own wounded heart by such beneficial spiritual practices as 'prayer, an offering, works of mercy, service of neighbour, voluntary self-denial, sacrifices, and above all the patient acceptance of the cross we must bear'. These natural responses of the healing heart are called, respectively, satisfaction and penance.[7] Neither is a condition of forgiveness, for there is no unforgiveness, only damage done to another and to the self: the healing heart longs to do what it can to restore that damage in both the self and the other, perfectly reflecting and cooperating with God's own desire for the same. In such cases of perfect contrition, the church does not presume to interfere: sacramental confession is available, but not required.[8]

The church recognises that there is also *imperfect contrition*. There is still 'a sorrow of the soul and detestation for the sin committed, together with the resolution not to sin again', but it arises less from 'a love by which God is loved above all else' and more from 'the consideration of sin's ugliness or the fear of eternal damnation and other penalties threatening the sinner'.[9] In cases of such imperfect contrition, the church invites the penitent to sacramental confession. This is an opportunity to receive the assurance of God's forgiveness, despite the imperfect contrition, and to discuss with the minister of the sacrament any appropriate satisfaction and penance, both aimed ultimately at restoring that 'love of God before all else'.[10]

In the particular case of mortal sin, even with perfect contrition, the church insists that the offender comes to sacramental confession – the sacrament of reconciliation – if there is to be a restoration of the relationship between the offender and the church.[11] This is as much about reconciliation with the church as with God, the offender having brought the institution into disrepute. Where there is contrition, even imperfect contrition, leading to some attempt at satisfaction and penance, the church assures God's forgiveness, and by this sacrament also declares reconciliation with the church community.

At no point is the sacrament of reconciliation about presuming to grant or withhold God's forgiveness. It is about the imperfectly contrite, and those guilty even of mortal sin, discussing their contrition, satisfaction, penance, and love for God with a minister of the church, and there receiving both reconciliation with the church and the assurance of God's forgiveness. It is a sacramental celebration of grace, forgiveness, and the healing of the wounded heart. Jesus' words to Peter about binding and loosing on earth having the same effect in heaven[12] are a warning about the use and abuse of these ordinary very human powers, not a granting of any new ones.

Universalism and the grace of purgatory

The ultimate power game played with sin and forgiveness is the threat of eternity in hell, which in many theologies is the majority destination. In contrast, all this abundant forgiveness points directly towards universalism: the confidence that all may enter heaven, and there is no hell.

This is not a doctrine to fear. It is not as if something terribly unfair is about to happen. The godly life is the best possible life here on earth, despite any superficial appearances to the contrary, so it matters not whether there is any heaven. If there is, the godly will be ready for it, the sinful will be in for a shock, and we shall all rejoice together. That shock is called purgatory: the simultaneous pain and joy of being a sinner looking into the face of God and being purged of all the harmful debris within ourselves that we have learned to detest - or will learn to detest in that moment. Saint Paul speaks of being purged or refined by fire like a precious metal: all that is bad in us will finally be burned away, and all that is good will live on in the presence of God.[13]

Sometimes I dare to believe that as each one meets face to face with ultimate reality - with Yahweh Elohim - at the moment of death, each one will recognise in the eyes of God the compassion they have been seeking all their lives, and run to it. Other times I suspect that even in that final moment some will look upon the ultimate reality which is God, and in a final act of arrogance, pride and contempt, turn away. The question of universalism is the question of how many people make this second choice.

The church affirms the free will in this final choice, and defines those who make it. 'To die in mortal sin without repenting' means to have committed evil - a grave matter executed with full knowledge and complete consent - and to have no trace of remorse, not even the fear or regret that define imperfect contrition.[14] This final choice is 'a radical possibility of human freedom, as is love itself'.[15] The consequence is defined only as separation from God,[16] so if God is the upholder of all life, the consequence is the end of life; the bible speaks not of eternal punishment, but of a fire that consumes the debris of those who have gone to the second death[17] and there just died, the sustaining compassion of their hearts destroyed. The question of universalism is whether all three conditions for mortal sin are ever fulfilled (grave matter, full knowledge, complete consent), and whether anyone, having reached that point, genuinely moves on with no hint of remorse or regret. The church advises that while 'we can judge that an act is in itself a grave offence, we must entrust judgement of persons' – that is, the status of their premeditation and subsequent remorse – 'to the justice and mercy of God'.[18] For the rest of humankind, where the compassion of the heart is merely wounded rather than destroyed, where there is any hint of contrition, in that final moment the heart both recognises and attains its perfect fulfilment in the infinite compassion of God.

In its most clear and explicit rejection of the punitive model, the church states that the negative consequences of sin for the sinner 'must not be conceived of as a kind of vengeance inflicted by God from without, but as following from the very nature of sin'.[19] Two negative consequences are defined: the eternal and the temporal. The eternal consequence is the damage done to the relationship with God: this is repaired, by God's grace, through contrition, and the infinite compassion of God. The temporal consequence is the 'unhealthy attachment to created things' that sin nurtures within us. Perfect contrition, where God is loved above all else, repairs the relationship with God, and undoes the unhealthy attachment to created things. With imperfect contrition, based on fear or regret, God is gracious, but we wilfully cling on to that unhealthy attachment to created things. All of that disappears in the final moment when we look upon God at the hour of our death. It is probably not helpful to think of the extent of that moment in earthly terms like minutes or hours or days, but that is the moment of purging, cleansing and perfecting, as our wilful foolishness melts away: it is a moment of perfect grace, finally letting go of our attachments to passing, material things, and converting our imperfect contrition of fear and regret into the perfection of love for God above all else.[20]

Sometimes as I contemplate these helpful notions I

momentarily imagine that I understand even indulgences - still there in the catechism[21] - as great public celebrations of penance, forgiveness, and successful detachment from created things, where we attain a profound communion with all those who have gone before.[22] But of this at least we can be sure: that there is no unforgiveness in God. The entire contemporary catholic theology of heaven, hell and purgatory is based on the image of a God of infinite compassion, who grants both grace and free will to humankind, even to the very end. At its most fundamental, it is about understanding and healing the damage we do to ourselves and to others, and restoring the harmony in our relationship with Yahweh Elohim, the ground of all being and the sum of all that is good.[23]

Ten Commandments

The ten commandments have often been assumed to be part of the legalistic and punitive model of sin: they have even been dismissed as a property code, devised in the service of the wealthy, in which wives are the property of their husbands, children are the property of their parents, and the grand conclusion (thou shalt not covet) is a warning not even to dream of rising above your appointed place in the social and economic hierarchy. In reality there are truths far more profound in the list of ten.

In Exodus chapter twenty it is Elohim (the gods) who speaks, saying, I am Yahweh Elohim, you will have no other gods (Elohim) before me; or possibly, just as validly, there are no other gods before me (that is, in existence anywhere).[24] This is an affirmation of the Yahweh Elohim principle, that when it comes to the ultimate essence of things, the sum of all divinity is one: an excellent way to begin the list of ten.

The Ten Commandments in eleven lines

Catholic and Lutheran usage has the second line implicit in the first. Anglican and protestant usage combines the last two lines. The traditional text is adapted from Exodus chapter twenty and Deuteronomy chapter five.

You shall have no other gods but me

You shall not make for yourself any idol

You shall not take the name of the Lord your God in vain

Remember the Sabbath day, and keep it holy

Honour your father and your mother

You shall not murder

You shall not commit adultery

You shall not steal

You shall not bear false witness

You shall not covet your neighbour's wife

You shall not covet your neighbour's goods

The first specific commandment is then a prohibition of the worship of any graven (carved or cast) image. Usually read as an arbitrary divine instruction on how to decorate or not decorate a temple, this is actually a profound warning against the idolatry of making God too small by comparing Yahweh Elohim to any earthly, created thing. It reminds us that God is beyond our imagining - unconstrained by any human category - and can warn us that even a metaphor for God is immediately in danger of diminishing God, making an idol of the metaphor. Idolatry is clinging on to created things, or a false image of God, in place of the ultimate mystery of

Yahweh Elohim. Inevitably it diminishes our hearts and lives.

Next comes the prohibition on taking the name of God in vain, a warning against presuming to speak in the name of God. Much harm and much evil has been done, some deliberately and some naively, by human beings claiming to speak on behalf of God. The abuse of the name of God down the centuries has had devastating consequences for individuals and entire cultures, and surely destroys the heart of the one abusing the name, even as it harms those who fall victim to the abuse. The warning against such abuse rightly appears on the list ahead of such straightforward misdemeanours as murder, adultery, theft and perjury.

Next in the sequence is the charge to 'remember the sabbath day and keep it holy'. Usually read as another arbitrary divine command, this could equally be read as good advice: take a day off, ideally with others, and take time out to remember Yahweh Elohim. Both are fundamental to preserving wellbeing.

The honouring of parents, next on the list, again need not be read as an arbitrary divine burden, placed even on those escaping from parental abuse. As a parish minister I saw the difference, amongst young parents, between those who had their own parents on hand to help and advise, and those whose own parents were hundreds of miles away; and for most of the rest of us, the older we become ourselves, the more we realise just how much our parents taught us. There is wisdom in honouring the judgement of those who have walked a particular path before, and there is wisdom in making a duty out of the mutual care that characterises the family bond. To have no regard for one's parents at all is to die a little.

The entire list can be read not as arbitrary commandment but as wise advice for living well. If we replace the censorious 'thou shalt not' with the equally valid 'you will not', and bring the original text's offer of a long and prosperous life from the middle to the front, the list sounds entirely valid and surprisingly contemporary. If you want to live well, a rich and fulfilled life, inheriting all the best gifts around you, you will not commit murder, adultery, theft or perjury, you will not waste time coveting your neighbour's spouse, you will not waste time coveting your neighbour's property, you will organise a sensible work-life balance for yourself and those immediately around you, you will take time to honour and celebrate the ground of all being and the sum of all divinity - allowing no limited religious concept to diminish it or come in its way - and you will not presume the authority to speak in the name of God.[25] The list is not arbitrary or inconvenient law, but wise counsel for living a rich and undiminished life.

Other models of sin

Elsewhere, in the Lord's Prayer, sin is understood as trespass or debt - the damage we do to one another[26] - and in the book of Proverbs, the great Old Testament book of collected wisdom, as folly or foolishness, the damage we do to ourselves.[27]

These two are one, for the more damaged we are within ourselves, the more we are a burden and a danger to others; the healthier we are within ourselves, the more positive our influence in the world.

The desert fathers (the early Christian monastic communities which gave us the Trinity and the creeds) recognised signs of this internal damage in their extensive work on the human condition, which enters the popular consciousness as the list of seven deadly sins: internal damage is recognised as sloth, anger, pride, envy, avarice, gluttony and lust. Pride is used here in its classic sense of overbearing self-importance, not in the modern sense of basic healthy self-esteem, something Jesus supported in all the down-trodden; avarice is hoarding and stinginess, in contrast to gluttony, which is excessive consumption, or any kind of excess; lust is not healthy human sexuality or the appreciation of human beauty, but the arrogance that reduces another human being to an object. All seven indicate the disintegration of the human condition from the ideal.[28]

Finally Jesus summed up 'all the law and the prophets' in just two commandments. They represent the ending of disintegration, and the finding of each person's true integrity, as human beings made in the image of a God who is love: 'Love Yahweh Elohim with all you mind, heart, soul and strength; and love your neighbour as yourself'.[29]

Integrity or Disintegration

To sin is not to break some arbitrary rule, incurring the wrath of an arbitrary God. To sin is to disintegrate: to lose our integrity, to damage the natural created compassion of the human heart.

God is not engaged in some struggle to overcome God's own wrath with a helping of forgiveness: God's only desire is to heal the damage that we inflict on ourselves and one another; and at no stage does God punish sin, for sin contains its own punishment.[30]

If we go with the flow of disintegration, our lives fall apart. If we aim instead for love and integrity, with heart and soul and mind and strength, there is a profound inner health where life abundant flourishes,[31] whatever superficial difficulties may befall.

Rites of Penance

I knew a minister who would begin every service or event

– however low key or informal – with a long extempore confession. Each time it would ramble on painfully towards the same conclusion: a pause, followed by the words, 'I'm sorry'. He sounded less like a beloved child being welcomed home, and more like an abused child standing before the abuser, in terror of some potential punishment; and yet it was only an extreme extempore version of the standard opening of virtually every protestant service in the world, including contemporary Church of England rites, recklessly or deliberately reinforcing the punitive model of sin. During my eleven years as the Church of England priest at Church Langley,[32] we used the shortest permitted alternative from the 1980 service book,[33] and still it had the potential to hang heavy, like a miserable dead weight, at the start of the service. At least it avoided the phrase 'we are truly sorry', present in all the others, and extended in one of them to 'we are sorry and ashamed'.

I did finally learn how to relate to the text: I began to use it with the formality of a creed, a statement of fact. 'Almighty God, our heavenly Father, we have sinned against you, through our own fault, in thought and word and deed, and in what we have left undone.' Sin is against God in that it damages God's perfect creation, and it wounds God's heart of compassion to see it. This statement I can acknowledge like a creed, but there is no need to grovel. The text moves straight on to a simple prayer: 'For your Son our Lord Jesus Christ's sake, forgive us all that is past, and grant that we may serve you in newness of life, to the glory of your name. Amen.' To insist week after week on the cringing emotional plea – 'we are truly sorry' – is not in the spirit of the gospel, and even detracts from the harshness of the more formal factual acknowledgement that begins the prayer.

The equivalent Roman Catholic text avoids the sorry plea altogether and ventures instead into another important area of acknowledgement: that we damage not only ourselves but also the community of which we are a part. The text once again takes the form of a statement - like a creed rather than a prayer - and dramatically is addressed not to God, but to the people around us. 'I confess to almighty God, and to you, my brothers and sisters, that I have sinned through my own fault, in my thoughts and in my words, in what I have done, and in what I have failed to do.' Rather than pleading with God for forgiveness, it asks for general prayer, from the community gathered around and from the saints who have gone before. 'I ask blessed Mary ever virgin, all the angels and saints, and you, my brothers and sisters, to pray for me to the Lord our God.' It is a text entirely in keeping with the model of sin as damage inflicted on ourselves and one another, with healing sought from a compassionate God, and forgiveness directly from our neighbours.

Unique to the anglican rite is the chillingly superior 'you' form of public absolution. After the confession, the priest prays not for 'us' all together, but for 'you' the penitent sinners. The church draws extra attention to this pretentious affectation by printing the prayer's five occurrences of the words 'you' and 'your' in italics. This is done to remind lay people reading the prayer that they are required to say 'us' and 'our' instead: only the priest is worthy to say 'you' and 'your'. The text is also a nonsense of syntax, addressed both to God and to the people. Perhaps it is giving God an order: 'Almighty God, who forgives all who truly repent, have mercy upon you'.[34] Once again the Roman Catholic text has it right. With priestly humility - and in seventeen words rather than thirtyeight - the priest simply responds to the request 'pray for me to the Lord our God'. 'May almighty God have mercy on us, forgive us our sins, and bring us to everlasting life.'

The problem of course is less the words we use and more what we believe. Protestantism, dominated by evangelicalism, especially in the English-speaking world, is locked into the punitive model: the board of the UK Evangelical Alliance - the main evangelical body in the UK - issued a statement in February 2006 affirming that belief in penal substitutionary atonement (the crucifixion inflicted on Christ as God's punishment for human sin) was a condition of membership, the logical conclusion of its core belief in God's wrath against all people on account of their sin.[35] In contrast, whatever the history of the Roman Catholic church in terms of compromise with secular powers and values, its contemporary catechism presents a God of infinite compassion, uncompromised by any trace of unforgiveness or wrath, and an understanding of sin as damage done to ourselves and to others that God longs only to heal.

The Final Doubt: not evil but failure

One final factor remains in the human experience of nagging guilt and low self-esteem: not the committing of sin, but the failure to do sufficient good.

Once again Jesus and the cross are our redemption, for Jesus also failed. The cross in particular represents spectacular public failure.

Jesus began his public ministry in the synagogue - a reformer within the established tradition - but he failed in this attempt at internal reform.[36] He was driven out of the synagogue in Nazareth,[37] and he took instead to preaching in private homes and public spaces.[38] Eventually he identified the established religious order as an enemy, making him a revolutionary rather than a reformer.[39] Public support for his radical agenda was at its politically most significant on Palm Sunday, when he was welcomed into Jerusalem by the crowds.[40] Just five days later he was dead, executed by the cooperation of the political and religious authorities. His mission had failed.

If our human god was an achiever of any kind - a Ghandi or a Mandela, a warrior or a king, a rags to riches entrepreneur or Cinderella - every one of us would be judged to be a failure in comparison. But our human god is not an achiever. Our human god is a spectacular failure: a failed reformer, and a failed revolutionary. To be truly and literally Christlike is not to succeed, but to fail spectacularly.

To have your heart in the wrong place is to sin, and there is forgiveness. To have your heart in the right place and to succeed is good - though the way is strewn with temptations, to pride and self-importance and self-righteousness. To have your heart in the right place and to fail spectacularly is to be truly, literally, Christlike: it is a vision of human divinity, a paradoxical human perfection, to which we can all aspire.

To fail as a parent, to fail as a spouse, to fail in a career or a ministry or a charity, to fail as a reformer or a leader or a mediator, to fail as a teacher or a carer or a social worker, to fail as an artist or an academic or a church volunteer: all of these achieve true Christlikeness, if only the heart is in the right place.

On the day that marks his definitive failure, the day of the crucifixion, Jesus is betrayed, denied and abandoned by his closest followers. If the existence of a church organised in his name today - in various forms two billion strong - is to be regarded as any kind of success, it was achieved not by Jesus himself but by the ordinary human beings who took it on and made it work in the days and weeks and months and years and centuries following. For the rest of us, to have failed spectacularly, but to have inspired just one other person in the effort - perhaps without even knowing it - is enough.

And the final guilty fear is that we could have done more of the less spectacular good: fed more of the hungry, tended more of the sick, as Jesus commends in the parable of the final judgement.[41]

Once again Jesus is our example, for sometimes even he would walk away. In the very first chapter of Saint Mark, they lay out the sick in the streets for him, but he has already gone into the hills alone to pray. They call him back, to attend to the sick, but he refuses, and presses on to the next town instead.[42] Sometimes we have other responsibilities, sometimes we just need to be alone; our finite, failing Jesus is our example, our salvation, and our God.

Chapter 3
Bible

Introduction

Many contemporary protestants, especially evangelicals, speak of the bible as though it were their God. They declare proudly that every decision in their lives is made subject to the bible. The bible is made the pre-eminent authority in all things, and declared to be the authentic and infallible Word of God.

This is a terrible idolatry, for the book is neither God nor the infallible Word of God. It was compiled by committees from a whole range of sources, and the question of what to include remained unresolved for centuries. There is no definitive text, and certainly no definitive translation. It only became widely available at all after the invention of the printing press, three quarters of the way through Christian history to date. It testifies to its various writers' supposed experiences of God, but it is not God, and should not be treated as God.

Anglican moderation speaks of three authorities interacting: scripture, tradition and reason. Anglican evangelicals speak of placing scripture at the apex of this triangle, with tradition and reason to be judged in the light of scripture. It is a scandal to suggest that human rationality - a divine gift to every human being - is to be forever subjugated to the authority of a book, prohibited from questioning or inquiring on any topic on which the book declares a view; and it is a practical nonsense to insist that tradition be judged in the light of the book, as the book itself is part of that ever-developing tradition: as recently as the sixteenth century, its compilation remained formally undefined, and Martin Luther sought to demote key New Testament texts like James and Hebrews to an appendix, primarily because he disliked their contents.[1] Still protestant leaders today wave their black leather bound, gilt edged compilations, proclaiming that every page, every line, has the full and unambiguous authority of God: that this alone is God's complete and perfect message to the world. Debate is then dominated by the degree of authority the bible should command. In such a highly charged atmosphere, it has become almost impossible to sustain an intelligent discussion about the actual text.

In order to look dispassionately at the actual contents of the bible, let us place reason at the apex of the triangle, and approach the book not as an authority, but as a potential resource, sifting through its contents as we have already sifted through some of the other resources of the western tradition, to determine whether there is anything here that might usefully enrich our understanding of Yahweh Elohim.

The bible as we receive it today is a hugely diverse collection, the work of hundreds of writers and compilers across more than a thousand years, who argue with each other and contradict each other as they apply their own limited human resources to the task of describing the great mystery which is God. The Old Testament specialises in saga, legend, myth, hagiography, poetry, parable and law; the New Testament in reportage and the collected writings of a handful of apostles. None of it was written with the intention of becoming part of the collection we call the bible - and unless we are confident in both Old Testament Hebrew and New Testament

Greek, we are also subject to the imprecise science of translation.

The Old Testament

The Old Testament, almost three quarters of the whole, relates to the time before Christ. It is divided into thirtynine separate works known as books. These in turn are divided into chapters, then further into separate lines known as verses. The first seventeen books recount the history: the creation, the stories of Abraham and his descendents, the giving of the law to Moses, the settlement of the promised land, the golden age under king David, the decline and fall of the nation, the exile in Babylon and the return to rebuild Jerusalem. The last seventeen are books of the prophets, active during the final phases of this history. Between these two sections are the five books known as wisdom or poetry. They are five of the most important books in the Old Testament, and three of them are virtually unknown.

Seventeen books of history and law

The first five books in the history section begin with creation and conclude with the entry into the promised land. They are known together as the Torah (law) or Pentateuch (five books). Throughout the five books the work of at least four different schools can be identified. Each of the four schools is a source of original material, or a significant editorial presence, as the text makes its way through the centuries into its present form. Each has its own distinctive literary style, and particular interests and perspectives. The four are known as the Yahwist, the Elohist, the Deuteronomist and the Priestly source, the first two on account of their preference for one of the names of God over the other, the Priestly source being

The Old Testament

The Pentateuch (five books):
Genesis, Exodus, Leviticus, Numbers, Deuteronomy.

Additional books of history:
Joshua, Judges, Ruth; Kingdoms (divided into four); Chronicles (divided into two); Ezra, Nehemiah, Esther.

Five books of poetry or wisdom:
Job, Psalms, Proverbs, Ecclesiastes, Song.

Seventeen books of the prophets
(the first five called major, the remaining twelve called minor):
Isaiah, Jeremiah, Lamentations, Ezekiel, Daniel; Hosea, Joel, Amos, Obadiah, Jonah, Micah, Nahum, Habakkuk, Zephaniah, Haggai, Zechariah, Malachi.

rather severe in theology and regulation, and the Deuteronomist having more the enthusiasm of a prophet.

Perhaps the most significant division within the Pentateuch is not the regular division into five books of approximately equal length (Genesis, Exodus, Leviticus, Numbers and Deuteronomy), but the distinctive nature of the first eleven chapters of Genesis in contrast to everything that follows. These first eleven chapters are pure saga, legend, myth, poetry and parable: two mutually incompatible creation stories, the expulsion from Eden, Cain and Abel, Noah's Ark, the Tower of Babel, three long genealogies, and the bizarre story of the giants or Nephilim, described as warriors and heroes of old, born to women who had been impregnated by sons of Elohim. After these legends of prehistory, the twelfth chapter of Genesis begins with the story of Abraham, who is far more likely to be an authentic historic figure, though shrouded now in hagiography, with his story endlessly manipulated for the benefit of whichever writer or editor had control of the text at the time. Abraham is the father of Isaac, and Isaac is the father of Jacob, whose name is changed to Israel. Jacob has twelve sons, the fathers of the twelve tribes of Israel. Amongst the twelve is Joseph. There is famine around the eastern Mediterranean and the entire extended family ends up in Egypt at the conclusion of the book of Genesis. Exodus opens four hundred years later with the Hebrew people reduced to slavery in Egypt. Moses leads them out of Egypt, through the Red Sea to Sinai, where they receive the law. A phenomenal amount of legal text, from many different hands, is added to the narrative at this point, aimed variously at the nomadic, agricultural and urban phases of the community's life. The entire book of Leviticus then consists of rules for the keeping of the Hebrew religion. The book of Numbers tells the story of forty years of wandering in the desert, including the spotting of giants (Nephilim) in chapter thirteen, and a talking donkey in chapter twenty-two. Finally Deuteronomy recounts Moses' address to the people the night before they enter the promised land.[2]

The supposed conquest of the promised land is incomplete and inconclusive, the story now of the book of Joshua. Four hundred years pass before Israel becomes a single united kingdom in the land: the heroes of the intervening period are given the generic title Judges, their stories recorded in the book of that name. The attractive short story of Ruth from this era is given a book of its own. There are then two accounts of the era of the kings, with the nation initially united under Saul, David and Solomon (reigning for forty years each), then divided into north (Israel) and south (Judah) until its final collapse and the exile in Babylon. The story is told in the book of Kingdoms and again in the later book of Chronicles, each with its own distinctive theological gloss on events. In our received text, Chronicles is divided arbitrarily in two, as the first and second book of Chronicles, and Kingdoms is divided into four, firstly into two as the arbitrarily named book of Samuel and book of Kings, and then into the first and second book of Samuel and the first and second book of Kings.[3] Finally in the history section, the books of Ezra and Nehemiah tell the story of the restoration of Jerusalem after the exile, and the book of Esther recounts one story of shrewd heroism during the exile.

The two key points of perspective for the telling of the story - and for the compiling of the laws - are the forty year reigns of the kings David and then Solomon in the tenth century BC, when the Hebrew people were a thriving and united nation, and the seventy year period of the exile in Babylon in the sixth century BC, when the exile forced on the Hebrew people a sense of unity and identity. The entire story is told or edited to suit the perspectives and purposes of these eras, with none of our modern concerns about literal historic accuracy or impartiality; the laws, likewise, belong to a particular society in the various stages of its development, defined and compiled for the needs of those eras. The most coherent single body of law is the book of Leviticus, a detailed religious law code. The New Testament repeatedly declares it obsolete and redundant: 'In speaking of a new covenant, God treats the first as obsolete, and what is becoming obsolete and growing old is ready to vanish away'; 'We are discharged from the law, so that we serve not under the old written code, but in the new life of the Spirit'.[4] The New Testament has great respect for the law as a concept, but is explicit in separating the Christian community from its detail.

Seventeen books of prophets

The seventeen books of the prophets - five called major,

twelve called minor - record the supposed words and works of prophets active during the division and decline of Israel, and the exile and restoration. Their tone is very different from the legalism and ritualism of the Torah, pleading with the people to care for the needy from a generous heart, and to remember their God: 'I desire steadfast love, not sacrifices; the knowledge of Elohim, not burnt offerings'.[5] The New Testament message - where a heart of love for God and neighbour is the first principle of a moral life - is more visible in the Old Testament prophets than in the Old Testament law.

Prophecy was never about predicting the future. Authentic prophecy is telling the truth about the present. The truth about the present may well include: 'If we carry on like this, disaster will come, but if we change our ways things will be better'; or, 'You can find inspiration by focusing on this glorious vision of the possible'; or, 'We need a saviour, and yet we are bound to mistreat him when he comes'.

Five books of poetry or wisdom

Between the seventeen books of history and the seventeen books of the prophets come the five books of poetry or wisdom, five of the most important books in the Old Testament. The book of Psalms - the best known of the five - provides some of the most important keys to New Testament faith in the entire Old Testament. All of human life is here, every emotion and every image of God, and yet many of these songs and prayers reflect an intimate and highly personal relationship between the psalmist and a Yahweh Elohim/Eloah who is recognisably the intimate and compassionate God of Jesus of Nazareth. The other four of the five could have come from any wisdom tradition anywhere in the world and anywhere in history. The books of Job, Proverbs, Ecclesiastes and

Song contain nothing distinctively Hebrew: no exodus, no law of Moses, no covenant with Israel, no history of the patriarchs, no prophets, no exile. They emerge from the great cultural melting pot which is the ancient middle east, with a single empire stretching at one stage from India to Ethiopia.[6] The so-called Wisdom of the East has been fashionable in the west since the 1960s, and much of it is right here in these neglected Old Testament texts, rich with resonances of Hinduism and Buddhism and more besides. Proverbs recites collected wisdom: advice for living well. Job is an argument over the concept of *karma,* concluding that those who suffer on earth are not necessarily suffering as a result of their own actions. Ecclesiastes considers the vanity of earthly wealth and pleasure in the face of sickness, sorrow, suffering and death, and advises full appreciation of the simple pleasures of life like simple food, useful work, and the companionship of a spouse. Song is an extended celebration of human sensuality and physicality - the bible's own miniature *kamasutram* - its most important aspect being its inclusion in scripture at all.[7]

A tour of world religions

The sheer diversity of material collected together into the Old Testament reflects every human emotion and every image of God. It has both universalism and tribalism, both legalistic and antinomian morality, both the principle that good deeds will be rewarded and the observation that often they are not, both monarchism and anti-monarchism, and even surviving hints of polytheism behind its monotheistic gloss.[8] There are so many different perspectives in this compilation that it might indeed merit the title The Word of Elohim - that is, of all religions.

Of course the text does not reach us as a deliberate

tour of world religions. The principle cause of the compilation is almost certainly the unity of the nation of Israel and the Hebrew people, firstly during the reigns of the kings David and Solomon, and later during the exile. It reaches us as one part compilation from diverse sources to one part convenient gloss. The notion of twelve tribes descended from twelve brothers is almost certainly an artificial construct aimed at forging a single stable nation out of diverse peoples, some of whom may previously have been nomadic, some of whom may have escaped from poor conditions or racial oppression in Egypt,[9] and some of whom may have had roots in Mesopotamia.[10] Abraham, Isaac and Jacob are as likely to be the unrelated ancient heroes of three different regions (like the later Judges) as three generations of one family, and the stories told of them may well fit into the same mythical category as those told in England of King Arthur and Saint George. Alongside the tidiness of the ten commandments lies an almost random collection of moral, ritual and cultural laws for nomadic, agricultural and urban communities, covering everything from religious dress to the details of what conditions to expect when selling your own daughter into slavery.[11] Particular recurrent tribal obsessions unrelated to the ten commandments include ritual food laws, male genital mutilation,[12] and child sacrifice, the active suppression of which is the most likely origin of the stories of Abraham's non-sacrifice of Isaac, the killing of every first-born Egyptian, and the special dedication to God of every first-born Hebrew male.[13]

Much of this celebrated history and law is morally ambiguous or morally repugnant, and yet there is a vast quantity of material here worth preserving, both within the history and beyond it in the wisdom books and the prophets. Recognising the material as saga, legend, myth, hagiography, poetry and parable allows that richness to be recovered. It is regrettable that this aspect of biblical scholarship appears to have virtually disappeared from the mainstream protestant churches. Instead, engagement with the text focuses on futile attempts to defend Old Testament conquest, tribalism and polygamy, a six day theory of creation, and the idea that Jonah was swallowed by a fish and lived to tell the tale. Until recently the UK largely managed to avoid such nonsense, but the growth of worldwide Christian fundamentalism now leaves most UK protestant leaders too embarrassed even to mention these topics, lest they be required to take a stance. Once again it is contemporary Roman Catholicism that is left to take an appropriate stand. The catechism virtually forbids the literal interpretation of the first three chapters of Genesis, describing the language as figurative.[14] 'These texts may have had diverse sources. The inspired authors have placed them at the beginning of Scripture to express in their solemn language the truths of creation – its origin and its end in God, its order and goodness, the vocation of humankind, and finally the drama of sin and the hope of salvation.' They are to be read 'in the light of Christ, within the unity of Sacred Scripture and in the living Tradition of the Church'.[15] Richard Holloway has helpfully described these chapters as 'good poetry, not bad science'. The logic of this form of analysis applies to the entire Old Testament text.

The New Testament

The New Testament consists of twentyseven separate works or books. Four compilations of the sayings and works of Jesus known as the Gospels are placed first, followed by an account of the life of the early church known as the Acts of the Apostles,[16] then thirteen collected works of Saint Paul ranging from grand thesis to routine correspondence, eight other works of apostles

The New Testament

Four Gospels: Matthew, Mark, Luke, John.

The Acts of the Apostles.

Thirteen letters of Saint Paul: Romans, Corinthians (2), Galatians, Ephesians, Philippians, Colossians, Thessalonians (2), Timothy (2), Titus, Philemon.

Eight further letters:
Hebrews, James, Peter (2), John (3), Jude.

The Revelation to Saint John the Divine.

similarly diverse, and finally Revelation, the apocalyptic vision of Saint John the Divine.

Beyond the law

Saint Paul's grand thesis is the letter to the Romans. Paul argues that for Jew and Gentile alike, the old life can now be replaced by new life in Christ.[17] The old life might have been characterised either by complete licence and lawlessness, or by futile attempts to keep to the letter of some legalistic code, but neither licentiousness nor legalism can lead to fullness of life, indeed each is as bad as the other. New life is made possible by Christ, in whom we are justified, by grace, through faith, not by law or good works. The new life in the spirit (*en pneumati*) is characterised by freedom: freedom from both legalism and licentiousness.[18] The letter to the Ephesians is a shorter version of the same material, a similar combination of grand thesis followed by practical advice and instruction.

Paul's resentment and loathing for legalism is at its most vehement in the earlier letter to the Galatians, where he roundly condemns those who would require Christians to submit to the Hebrew religious code, but in Romans he attempts (and struggles) to rehabilitate the Hebrew legalistic tradition as an earlier stage in God's plan. Part of the struggle is language: Paul has no word for ethics other than law. Paul's own journey, and his commendation to others, is to move from the futility of following defined rules for right and wrong behaviour to following underlying principles like the principle of universal compassion - which can overrule individual laws - and ultimately to life in the spirit, following the perfect will of God alone.

Amongst Paul's other letters, the letter to the Philippians, written from prison, is a very personal meditation on joy. The first of two letters to the Corinthians attempts to address their exuberant charismatic style without crushing it entirely, a section that concludes with the glorious hymn to love;[19] the second is exasperated and whinging in comparison, but all the letters contain inspiring moments, often in the opening sections. After their opening sections, the two letters to the Thessalonians address the practical chaos caused by some who were disengaging from the present world in the anticipation of its early demise, the letter to the Colossians goes on to address an obsession with rituals and with visions of angels (both deemed irrelevant next to the centrality of Christ), the letter to Philemon is little more than a short personal note, and finally two letters to Timothy and one to Titus contain practical advice for the ongoing life of rather more stable church communities.[20]

The other grand thesis of the New Testament, alongside the letter to the Romans, is the letter to the Hebrews. It does not name its author, and there are many theories: it is not Paul, as the literary style is far more polished and poetic than Paul's; one possibility is the

New Testament figure Apollos, a scholar from Alexandria with a thorough knowledge of the Hebrew scriptures, whose speciality in preaching is 'proving from the scriptures that Jesus is the Christ'.[21] Apollos is respected by Paul, and influential alongside Paul in Corinth, with some believers there pledging loyalty to one over the other.[22] The letter to the Hebrews draws heavily on images and ideas from the Hebrew scriptures, stressing continuity with the faith of the Old Testament, but presenting Jesus as fulfilling and exceeding Old Testament hopes and promises and replacing Old Testament ways. As in Romans, the Old Testament law is respected, but declared to be superseded.[23] Hebrews also has an important role, alongside the gospel and letters of John, in emphasizing both Jesus's full humanity and his full divinity: Jesus is involved in the creation and preservation of the universe, and bears the very imprint of God's nature, being Son and heir to God,[24] but he also shared in our own flesh and blood,[25] being human in every respect, including suffering and temptation, that he might be a merciful and faithful high priest as one from amongst us.[26] It is the movement from the highest heaven to full humanity and back that makes Jesus Messiah,[27] Saviour, and God; born in our own flesh and blood, he leads the way that we might follow.

The rest of the New Testament letters bear familiar gospel names: Peter, James, John and Jude.[28] There are debates about authenticity and later editorial work, and even the possible combination of material from various sources, but in each case the letters emerge from the early church in their present form, and are deemed worthy of inclusion in the compilation which is the New Testament. The letter of James resembles the Old Testament wisdom literature, or Jesus's Sermon on the Mount,[29] as a series of wise sayings and instructions. The letters of Peter seem to be familiar with the theology of both Romans and

Hebrews (or perhaps directly with both Paul and Apollos) and contain exhortations to faith and good practice. The letters of John, like the gospel of John, focus on the virtue of love within the Christian community. The short letter of Jude resembles the second letter of Peter. Finally the Revelation to Saint John presents a vision of heaven and the end of time, with Christ at its centre.

All of this diverse material is consistent on the emerging doctrine of Christ as both fully human and fully divine. The identifiable argument within the text lies elsewhere, and is thoroughly contemporary: the default religious position based on law and punishment stands in continuous tension with the radical new proclamation of spiritual liberation through freedom from religious law.

The tension between law and freedom is perhaps most evident within Saint Paul, who retains a lingering admiration for the rigour of the law behind his confident condemnation of the harm it does and its ultimate futility. James takes issue with Paul's suggestion that faith is sufficient on its own, arguing that faith will inevitably lead to a more moral life, including charitable good works, and that if it does not do so, it is no faith at all,[30] and yet there is no disagreement on substance here, only on emphasis: Paul himself implies that faith will lead to a higher moral standard in his occasionally intemperate attacks on all manner of licentious lives,[31] and in his expectation of charity amongst the faithful.[32]

The issue comes to a head at the Council of Jerusalem, described fairly objectively by Saint Luke in the Acts of the Apostles chapter fifteen, and rather more feistily by Saint Paul in Galatians chapter two. The purpose of the council is to determine the obligations to be placed upon gentile converts. Paul and Barnabas report that gentile believers have received the gifts of the Holy Spirit in exactly the same way as Jewish believers, despite having been placed under no obligation to commit to the law of

Moses, and having no intention of doing so. The council therefore resolves, on the basis of the evidence, that God, by God's own action, has declared commitment to the law of Moses to be unnecessary for the new life in the Spirit.[33]

The Gospels

Placed ahead of these collected New Testament works are the four compilations of the sayings and works of Jesus himself known as the gospels.

The first three gospels - Matthew, Mark and Luke - contain much of the same material as each other, and the study of their inter-relation is a science all of its own. Mark is the shortest overall, but for the stories it does contain, it has the longest versions: the same stories in Matthew and Luke seem to have been abbreviated virtually sentence by sentence. Matthew and Luke therefore contain a huge amount of additional material, some of it unique to each of them, some of it common to them both, although often arranged differently. This additional material includes extensive compilations of the sayings of Jesus, including The Sermon on the Mount in Matthew and The Sermon on the Plain in Luke.[34] In the end we can only guess at the processes behind these final compilations of material, but the end result in each case is a highly polished presentation of the life, sayings and works of Jesus. Matthew's presentation of the material seems to be aimed primarily at a Jewish audience, presenting Jesus as the perfect teacher, the new law-giver, and the foundation of a new covenant with God. Luke appears to speak more confidently to the wider gentile audience, presenting Jesus as the universal saviour.

The final gospel, Saint John's, has a very different style from the other three, and possibly a different purpose: its language is more poetic, there is very little material in common with the other gospels apart from the account of the trial and the crucifixion, and key elements like the baptism of Jesus and the institution of the eucharist are missing. It has been suggested that this gospel is less an account of the life of Jesus, and more a series of sermons or meditations, assuming familiarity with the story itself. Compared to the apparent theological reticence of the other gospel accounts, John emphasises both Jesus's humanity and his divinity, his role as Son of God.

The Realm of the Divine

At the heart of Jesus's ministry is the invitation to commit not to any earthly kingdom, but to the realm of the divine: to the kingdom of the air and of the sky. The concept follows naturally from a confidence in Yahweh Elohim as *abba pater*, our generous and compassionate God, and leads directly to every other aspect of Jesus's teaching and ministry.[35]

The phrase 'Kingdom of God' is tarnished by abuse - conjuring up images harsher than any earthly regime - but its original use was to contrast, not to liken. *Basileia,* translated as kingdom, is an abstract noun from the outset, meaning reign or rule or extent of influence: *basileia theos* is the realm of the divine. Saint Matthew's preferred *basileia ouranos* we can render as the kingdom of the air or the kingdom of the sky, even more clearly in deliberate contrast to the kingdoms of the earth.

The first proclamation of the new agenda - by John the Baptiser (John the Baptist) and then by Jesus himself - is 'Repent, for the Kingdom of Heaven is at hand'.[36] In routine evangelical and protestant language, this gracious invitation has been made into a menacing threat, a call to list all your sins and prepare your defence in the face of a wrathful God. In its original context it is not a threat but a generous invitation: 'You can turn your life around, because the realm of the divine is right here'; the Greek *metanoia,* for repent, means turn around.

The Sermon on the Mount

After four chapters of preamble and introduction, Matthew's gospel sets out the central themes of the teaching of Jesus in chapters five to seven, the section known as The Sermon on the Mount. This compilation of sayings sets the agenda for everything that follows.

The section begins with the Beatitudes or blessings, turning earthly values upside down: the truly blessed are not the powerful, the proud, the warmongers or the arrogant, but the meek, those who mourn, those who hunger and thirst for righteousness, the merciful, the pure in heart, the peacemakers. These are truly the children of God, the salt and light of the earth, to whom all good things belong: mercy, comfort, fulfilment, a vision of God, and the kingdom of the air and of the sky.[37]

There follows a quotation - in Matthew's gospel only - that can be controversial out of context. Jesus asserts that he has not come to abolish the law and the prophets. Presumably by the time he makes this statement he has been accused of seeking to do so.

Fundamentalists worldwide have taken this quotation out of context and used it to justify their passionate devotion to their own arbitrary subset of Old Testament law. Placed back in context, the quotation serves to introduce the section that follows, in which Jesus uses the same poetic structure repeatedly to illustrate that the Old Testament law asks too little of us. What Jesus demands is far more: not merely to avoid murder, but to avoid anger; not merely to avoid adultery, but to avoid unhealthy, objectifying lust; not merely to limit vengeance to like-for-like ('an eye for an eye and a tooth for a tooth'), but to overcome evil with good; not merely to do what is required of us, but to do more, and with a generous heart; not merely to love your neighbour, but to love your enemy. In these ideals there is a perfection the law can never achieve: the perfection of your *pater en ouranois*, your father in the skies, who makes the sun rise on the evil and the good alike, and provides rain for both the unjust and the just.[38]

Having established this principle - that the law is not enough - Jesus roundly condemns the hypocrisy of the religious leaders of his day, who show off their piety in public, sound the trumpet as they enter the temple, stand praying on the street corners, and look deliberately miserable when they fast. They have built their lives on useless foundations - sand instead of rock - and though they plead that they have worked and spoken boldly in the name of God, God will say, 'I do not know you'.[39]

The analysis applies to the proudly religious in every age, including our own. Jesus warns for the future, 'Beware of false prophets, who come to you in sheep's clothing, but inwardly are ravenous wolves,' and offers for discernment: 'You will know them by their fruits'.[40] By the standards of the Sermon on the Mount so far, we look for meekness, mercy, a peaceful spirit, humility, love for enemies, and a trusting confidence in God alone, in preference to anger, revenge, hatred, and any show of public piety. The ultimate challenge is 'Judge not, that you be not judged; for with the judgement you pronounce you will be judged, and the measure you give will be the measure you receive'. Judgementalism belongs to those who ultimately condemn themselves, and not to the children of the sky.[41]

Those who choose to belong to the realm of the divine invest the heart not in earthly treasure ('where moth and rust destroy, and thieves break in and steal') - but in treasure that lasts, trusting *pater en ouranois* to provide for our earthly needs without anxiety or fear. The treasure of the realm of the divine has already been defined: meekness, mercy, a peaceful spirit, humility, universal love and trust in Elohim. Seek these first, and all earthly needs will follow.[42]

Matthew eight to fourteen

Having established the core teachings of Jesus as the foundation for all that follows, in the next seven chapters Matthew offers a flavour of Jesus's three years of public ministry.

In chapters eight and nine, we see Jesus's generous interactions with a whole range of individuals, and his radical disregard for established social structures and expectations in his uncompromising prioritisation of the realm of the divine.[43] In chapter thirteen we hear a whole series of parables describing the presence, growth and influence of the realm of the divine, the kingdom of the air and of the sky: it is like seed scattered on good soil and bad alike; it is like a tiny seed that becomes a great bush or tree; it is like hidden treasure in a field, or the yeast in the dough; it is like good seed competing with vigorous weeds, which grow side by side until the harvest. As early as chapter ten Jesus is sending out the disciples to replicate his ministry throughout the region. By the end of this section in chapter fourteen he is speaking to a gathered crowd of more than five thousand. There are healings and other miracles - of which more later[44] - and there are early hints of the controversy being stirred by Jesus's ministry amongst the official religious leaders of the time. This comes to a head in chapter twelve: one of the most strictly observed religious rituals of the time was the rigorous keeping of the sabbath, but Jesus and his disciples have little interest in such ritualistic piety. Walking through a field of ripe grain on the sabbath, they pluck some heads of grain and eat, and the Pharisees see their chance to condemn. Jesus uses their own scriptures to expose the vacuous nature of their religious demands, then deliberately taunts them by performing a healing on the sabbath in the public forum of the synagogue. They accuse Jesus of being in league with the devil, and Jesus responds with words no less forthright, suggesting that in their purity and pride they have been possessed by seven demons worse than the one they first drove out. They go out 'and take counsel against him, how to destroy him'.[45]

Matthew fifteen to seventeen

Two key turning points in Matthew's gospel now follow, after which the story turns altogether darker, with a persistent sense of the gathering storm that will become the ultimate darkness and desolation of Good Friday.

The first turning point is Jesus's encounter with a gentile woman in chapter fifteen.[46] It follows a dialogue between Jesus and the Pharisees[47] in which Jesus reaches the logical conclusion of his new approach to religious law. Challenged about his failure to observe the laws regarding ritual cleansing before eating, Jesus condemns the pedantry of the Pharisees as a hypocrisy which honours God with words but not with the heart. He goes on to condemn the entire system of food laws - fundamental to Hebrew daily life - 'for it is not what goes into the mouth that defiles you, but what comes out.' What goes into the mouth 'goes into the stomach then passes on', but what comes out of the mouth 'comes from the heart - evil thoughts, murder, fornication, theft, false witness, slander: these are what defile you, not eating with unwashed hands'. For the first time Jesus explicitly condemns an entire tranche of Hebrew law. He may have taken even himself by surprise, thinking aloud in the lucidity of his anger at the hypocrisy of his detractors.

This logical conclusion about the role of the Hebrew law is then immediately put to the test. A gentile woman pleads for healing for her daughter, and Jesus, still seeing his role as a reformer within the Hebrew tradition, dismisses her: 'I was sent only to the lost sheep of the house of Israel; it is not fair to take the children's bread and throw it to the dogs'. The woman challenges him: 'Yes Lord (*kurios*), but even the dogs eat the crumbs that fall from the master's (*kurios*) table'. Jesus replies, 'O woman, great is your faith, be it done for you as you desire'.

The significance here is not the granting of the gentile woman's request, but Jesus's realisation that if the Hebrew law brings no benefit, the gentiles are the Hebrews' equals in the realm of the divine. The renunciation of the food laws and the encounter with the gentile woman together represent a turning point in Jesus's human understanding of his message and his role.

The story of the feeding of the four thousand follows. This is a reference to the gentiles, who are now invited to join the new community of the realm of the divine. The number five, as in the previous feeding of the five thousand with five loaves, refers to the Hebrew tradition presented in the five books of the Pentateuch. The numbers four and seven, in the feeding of the four thousand with seven loaves, refer to the gentiles, imagined as seven nations from the four points of the compass. The great feast of the kingdom - the kingdom of the air and of the sky - is joined by the gentiles on equal terms. To conclude the section, Jesus warns the disciples to beware of the poisonous influence of the Pharisees and the Sadducees,[48] the upholders of the legalistic tradition.[49]

The next major turning point follows immediately here in chapter sixteen. Perhaps by now the fully human Jesus is genuinely concerned at where the logic of his teaching and his ministry is leading. He asks his disciples -

because he genuinely wants to know – 'Who do people say that I am'. They offer answers that reveal the seriousness of the discussions already going on: John the Baptist come back to life, or even one of the ancient prophets like Elijah or Jeremiah.

'And you,' asks Jesus, 'who do you say that I am?'

Perhaps Jesus has already wondered about the reply that Peter now gives, but never quite allowed the words to form in his own mind. Peter replies, 'You are the Christ,[50] the Son of the living God (*theos* / Elohim).' Jesus replies, 'Do not say that, do not say that to anyone'.[51]

From this point onwards the gospel takes on a consistently darker tone, with Jesus talking regularly about the opposition his ministry faces, and the inevitable consequences of that opposition. Peter challenges this dark assessment, and Jesus rebukes him for his lack of insight, warning all the disciples that following him now means surrendering life in order to gain it.[52]

In chapter seventeen, the insights of the previous chapter are confirmed to Peter, James and John in the vision known as the Transfiguration. They see Jesus bathed in light, talking with Moses and Elijah, then hear a voice from the light: 'This is my beloved son, listen to him'. The disciples fall with their faces to the ground, and the vision fades. It is the familiar Jesus who now touches them gently, reassures them, and asks them to tell no-one – for now – of what they have seen. The new darker mood is then reinforced as the disciples fail in an attempted healing. Jesus intervenes, then warns them a second time of the persecution that now lies ahead.

Matthew eighteen to twenty

There are just three more chapters of teaching and ministry before the entry into Jerusalem. Chapter eighteen continues the teaching about the kingdom of the air and of the sky. It is a place where the greatest is not the one who seeks power but the one who has the simple trust of a child; where every lost soul is sought and welcomed home; where peace is sought between individuals, not least through generous forgiveness, if only as an acknowledgement of the forgiveness that we ourselves receive. Chapter nineteen contains darker challenges on the responsibility of marriage and the burden of wealth, leading the disciples to speculate that it may be expedient not to marry at all, and Jesus to observe that it is easier for a camel to pass through the eye of a needle[53] than for a rich man to embrace the realm of the divine and the kingdom of the air and of the sky. Finally in chapter twenty Jesus presses home one of the basics: that there is absolute equality amongst individuals in the realm of the divine and the kingdom of the sky. There is no extra benefit for those who join first, indeed on earth there will be suffering. 'You know that the rulers of the nations lord it over them. It shall not be so amongst you. If you wish to be great, be a servant. If you wish to be first, be a slave.'

Holy Week – Matthew twenty-one to twenty-eight

With chapter twenty-one we enter the final days known as Holy Week. As the crowds gather for a major religious festival, Jesus turns his own arrival in Jerusalem into a public spectacle. Perhaps by now he has no choice, if the word on the streets is that the controversial Galilean[54] is on his way; or perhaps this is Jesus seizing his own destiny: either way, the details of the event are entirely Jesus's own. The timing is already provocative. The decision to enter the city on a donkey is both provocative and subversive: Jesus is hailed by those present as a king, while riding a donkey like a working peasant. Behind the drama, Jesus would be fully aware of the relevant prophecy in the book of Zechariah, and those observing with contempt would be fully aware that he was fully aware. 'Rejoice, O Jerusalem. Behold, your king comes to you, triumphant and victorious, humble and riding on the foal of a donkey'.[55]

From the very beginning it is a week of high tension and controversy. In a deliberate and pre-meditated act,[56] Jesus causes very public chaos in the temple, overturning the tables of the money-changers and driving out the traders, all justified by quoting Isaiah and Jeremiah.[57] There are continuous public arguments with the established religious leaders, to which Jesus replies with pointed parables: one son spurns his father's authority, but does the right thing anyway, while another pledges allegiance but is idle; a vineyard is left in the care of tenants who behave disgracefully, until it is taken from them and given to others.[58]

Finally in chapter twenty-three there is open denunciation of the scribes[59] and Pharisees for their hypocrisy: they make God inaccessible; they make converts worse than themselves; they are pedants in the detail of the law who neglect the greater issues of justice, mercy and faith. They strain out a gnat and swallow a camel; they polish the outside of the cup ignoring the filth inside; they are white-washed tombs, shining without, putrid within. There are thirty-nine verses of this, concluding more in sorrow than in anger, as Jesus mourns over the consequences for the Jerusalem he loves.

In chapter twenty-four Jesus speaks of the tragedies that lie ahead: of famines, earthquakes and wars; of false prophets, false religions, the destruction of the temple; of persecutions, days of global tragedy, a loss of faith, and love growing cold. Like all authentic prophecy, this is not prediction, just the truth about how things are and how they will be. Chapter twenty-five has related parables about the final day, the end of the age. In chapter twenty-six the familiar sequence begins that moves relentlessly towards the crucifixion: the anointing at Bethany, the last supper, the prayer in Gethsemane, the arrest and trial, Peter's denial; and in chapter twenty-seven, the crucifixion, death and burial. Chapter twenty-eight concludes with Matthew's resurrection stories and the new beginning.[60]

Legalism and Licence

The tragedy of the contemporary debate between protestant fundamentalism and protestant liberalism is that the actual contents of the bible are ignored by both sides. The fundamentalists present the book as a collection of laws to be obeyed. The liberals fail to challenge this trivial assessment, and argue instead that the book has no contemporary significance. Neither side is engaging with the text itself: instead they have become the two diametrically opposed parties Saint Paul describes in defining the old life without Christ. The fundamentalists are the legalists, for ever accusing others and proclaiming their own righteousness while ignoring the vast majority of biblical laws and formulating their own instead. The liberals are the licentious, with no law at all beyond a vague sense of guilty obligation or propriety - consequently climbing on any fashionable ethical bandwagon.

The legalists - the fundamentalists - are the more soundly condemned in the New Testament, being equivalent to the New Testament Pharisees with their pedantic observation of their chosen set of laws, their self-righteousness, and their ready condemnation of others. It is a hypocrisy which honours God with words and superficial deeds but not with the heart;[61] they plead that they have worked and spoken boldly in God's name, but God replies, 'I do not know you';[62] they make God inaccessible, they make converts worse than themselves, they are pedants in detail who neglect the greater issues of justice, mercy and faith;[63] they are possessed by seven demons worse than the one they first cast out.[64] We are to beware of their poisonous influence.[65]

At the opposite end of the scale, complete licence or licentiousness – life with no sense of structure or ethics or purpose – is equally self-destructive. The New Testament's ethical structure is not licentiousness, but the complex liberation of the single law of love. It is the call to universal compassion, characterised by universal forgiveness and by love even of enemies, with the teaching and ministry of Jesus providing idealistic and practical examples, from compassion for the outcast to the washing of the disciples' feet.[66] The ultimate New Testament challenge is life in the Spirit: every moment lived in the presence of the God who is infinite compassion.

The Old Testament serves as a tour of world religions, containing the best and the worst of all that exists in religion and spirituality. The New Testament is then the foundation of a new spirituality based not on any religious law, but on freedom from all earthly law – including all religious law – because God is no wrathful king, but is *abba pater*, infinite compassion. We are called to live *en Christo* (in Christ), and *en pneumati* (in the Spirit), in the realm of the divine, in the kingdom of the air and of the sky, free from both self-destructive licentiousness and hypocritical law, reaching instead for the higher ideal of the universal compassion which is Yahweh Elohim, the ground of all being and the sum of all divinity.

Scripture and Liturgy

For protestants, the bible is an ultimate authority: its

exists primarily is as a book of law. Defining the boundaries and meaning of the text are tasks essential to the religion, of which this one book is supposedly the foundation, and within which it has the status of a deity.

For catholics, holy scripture ('that which is written') exists primarily as a part of the liturgy. The concept of a formally compiled bible emerged after, not before, the idea of deciding which texts could appropriately be read as holy scripture at mass. Those texts were not drawn from a pre-defined bible: that hypothetical bible existed only as the compilation of those texts. In the catholic model the holy scriptures are naturally interwoven into the life of the community, rather than standing apart from it as an overlord. The catholic model is also more true to the history: Jesus did not write a book, but founded a community; the community wrote the book.

The various forms of scripture have different roles within the mass. A reading from the gospels is so central to the mass that everybody stands, as Christ is made present once again in the recounting of these words and deeds. Matthew, Mark and Luke are read sequentially, Sunday by Sunday, each with its own year in a three year cycle. Extracts from Saint John fit in around the edges, taking dates in Lent and Eastertide, and in the year of Mark.[67] Another New Testament scripture is read each Sunday in addition to the gospel, also reading in sequence from week to week for most of the year. The Old Testament is treated differently: Old Testament texts are not read in sequence from Sunday to Sunday; instead, each Sunday has a first reading selected from anywhere in the Old Testament - law, history, wisdom, prophecy, or apocrypha - to complement and illustrate the Gospel reading for the day. This method for selecting the Old Testament reading is the practical expression of a theological principle: that the primary texts of the Christian faith are the Gospels and the rest of the New

Testament, with the Old Testament serving to illustrate, not to dictate. Psalms are also used, either read or sung, also chosen to complement or illustrate the Gospel and Old Testament theme for the day.[68]

This supposed demotion of the Old Testament is shocking to some protestants, who are used to regarding the bible as a clearly defined seamless whole from one leather cover to the other. As a consequence, the protestant adaptation of the Roman Catholic system, now in widespread use in protestant denominations worldwide, also reads extracts from Old Testament sagas sequentially, Sunday by Sunday, for at least half the year. This includes material that we have previously described as morally ambiguous or morally repugnant.[69]

Protestant translation

For protestants, the book itself is far more important than its liturgical use. In practice, this means their own particular interpretation of, or assertions and assumptions about, the book itself: these they will declare to be the only possible interpretations of a bible supposedly consistent and infallible in Old Testament and New. Having given the book the status of a deity, they can then manipulate that deity through the imprecise sciences of translation and interpretation, assisted by countless unexamined assertions and assumptions. Many modern protestant bibles are privately mocked by scholars for being not so much translations of the original texts as evangelical commentaries upon them.

The liberties taken by translators can be extreme in their effects. Romans chapter four is a closely argued chapter in which Saint Paul establishes that it was faith in God, not obedience to the law, that characterised the most important Old Testament heroes. The passage is part of

Paul's case against legalism, which he denounces as worthless and dangerous. The point of the argument is that God cares about faith, not law.

In verse fifteen, Saint Paul makes the observation that legalism tends to generate anger (*katergazomai* - to bring about, result in, accomplish, achieve). It is an observation we can affirm from our own experience of daily life. The verse does not mention God.

A survey of contemporary protestant translations reveals the following. In the Worldwide English New Testament: 'Because of the law, God is angry'. In the New International Reader's Version: 'The law brings God's anger'. In the Contemporary English Version: 'God becomes angry when his Law is broken'. In the New Life Version: 'God's anger comes on a man when he does not obey the Law'.

These statements are fully concordant with the evangelical doctrine of a wrathful God, but directly contrary to Saint Paul's own intention in writing the text. These loosely translated bibles are not of merely academic interest, for protestantism makes the text a deity. It was this kind of loose translation, in the service of an external agenda, that led to the Roman Catholic church seeking to suppress all unauthorised vernacular translations early in the reformation era.

The Revised Standard Version (RSV, 1952), and the more readable New Revised Standard Version (NRSV, 1989), remain the most authoritative English-language translations of the original texts.[70] In researching for the present project, I have even come to recognise the value of the virtually unreadable English-language Authorised Version (the King James Bible of 1611), when used alongside the original Hebrew and Greek texts, as a doggedly literal, word by word rendering of the originals. At Romans 4:15, RSV and NRSV have 'The law brings wrath'. The Authorised Version has the even more literal

'The law worketh wrath'. As in the original, there is no mention of God.

The Homily

Preaching is practiced in both catholic and protestant churches, although catholicism is more familiar with the five minute homily than the twenty, forty or sixty minute sermons of the protestant tradition. This universal practice of preaching would seem to contradict the spirit of the protestant doctrine of *sola scriptura* (the assertion that the bible alone is sufficient for salvation), as preachers seek to supplement the bible's offerings with their own week after week. A catholic liturgy in contrast contains more scripture, more structured and systematic use of scripture, and fewer words on top.

The church has always issued teaching and documents of various kinds to supplement scripture, from the earliest creeds, through the various declarations of the reformation era (both catholic and protestant), to contemporary preaching. The *Catechism of the Catholic Church,* commissioned by Pope John Paul II in 1986 and published in 1992, is an official authoritative and comprehensive compilation of church teaching, assembled and published as part of the church's ongoing response, decade by decade, to the agenda set by the Second Vatican Council (1962-1965) - and the first comprehensive compilation of church teaching in the church's history. Across its 800 pages, it manages to be simultaneously accessible, thorough and profound: an incomparable resource for the exploration of all aspects of the western spiritual tradition from the earliest times. It is not holy scripture, but it is an accessible and authoritative record of the faith, life and teaching of the church. Its clarity and accessibility are startling next to the often inconclusive and obscure contributions of the bible itself.

When it comes to understanding the richness of the western spiritual tradition, the bible alone is not enough.

Chapter 4
Creed

Nicaea and Constantinople

In many languages the word for believing shares a common origin with the word for glue. It comes through in English in the words adhesive and adherent. Belief is not knowledge, it is the model to which we adhere: we choose what to believe, and we cling to it. This is the nature of our creed: it sets out the life-changing choices we have made. Once we have chosen to work with a Trinitarian model - with Yahweh Elohim as infinite compassion and Jesus of Nazareth as its incarnation - the rest of the creed follows on.

The creed recognised by all mainstream Christian denominations as the definition of Christian orthodoxy is the creed adopted at Nicaea in AD325 and revised at Constantinople in AD381.[1] In the original Greek this revised Nicene Creed runs to 174 words; in English translation it runs to about 220. Its two key terms are *homoousion* and *enanthropesanta*. *Homoousion* describes the relationship of Jesus and the Father as 'being of the same substance', making Jesus fully divine. *Enanthropesanta* clarifies *sarkothenta*: *sarkothenta* is merely made physical or bodily; *enanthropesanta* is made human (*anthropos*).

Much of the rest is already familiar: there is one God (*theos*) who is both *pater* and *pantokrator* (all powerful, or the sum of all powers), as well as maker or fashioner (*poieten*) of the earth and the sky. Jesus is *kurios* and *christos* as well as only (*monogene*) son of God, begotten (*gennethenta*) not made (*poiethenta*), and *homoousion* (of one substance) with the Father. The relationship is described poetically as light from light (*phos ek photos*), the phrase used when one candle is lit from another: once they are both alight, it is impossible to tell which came first, as they now have the same nature (*homoousion*). The metaphor is clarified in a poetic repetition: light from light, true God from true God (*theon alethinon ek theou alethinou*). This process took place when the Son was begotten of the Father before the beginning of time (*gennethenta pro panton ton aionon*), allowing the twin metaphor whereby Christ is eternally both fully God and Son of God. Finally Holy Spirit (*pneuma hagion*) is also *kurios,* and giver of life, who spoke by the prophets, and is co-worshipped and co-glorified with the Father and the Son.

The Return

The text includes a short past and future biography of the Christ, and it is here that classic liberal objections have most commonly been made: not to the coming down from heaven for the salvation of humankind, the crucifixion under Pontius Pilate, or the death and burial, but to birth from the Virgin Mary, the resurrection, and the return ('he will come again in glory to judge the living and the dead, and his kingdom will have no end').

The return functions primarily as an expression of hope and confidence: that at the end of time, Yahweh Elohim will not be defeated, but will endure. For Trinitarians, this Yahweh Elohim incorporates the Christ, so the end of the world is described not as unmitigated disaster but as the triumphant return of Christ in glory. The end of the world was regarded as inevitable: the political and economic situation was perpetually precarious and brutal, there were wars and rumours of wars, and there was the fear of all manner of incomprehensible natural disasters. In our own time, the end of the world remains inevitable: even if humankind has moved elsewhere by the time the earth is swallowed up by the sun, this universe will come to an end in the final logical outworking of the big bang that started it all, in either the big chill, when all the energy is so dispersed that the entire universe goes cold, or the big crunch, when gravity finally reverses the universe's current ongoing expansion and everything collapses back into one infinitesimally small crushed ball, the ultimate black hole. The doctrine of the return of Christ holds that in that final moment, there is still Yahweh Elohim: still hope and faith and love, still the ideal of humankind, and still Jesus of Nazareth as the icon of the best that the universe has been. At the end, when all else has passed away, Yahweh Elohim and the glory of Christ remain; and in our own time, the direction of the universe is towards glory and not disaster.[2]

The Resurrection

The resurrection of Jesus two days after the crucifixion ('on the third day') was a mystery at the time, and is reported as such in the gospels. The disappearance of the body from the tomb is reported by all four gospel writers.[3] It sets the scene for the accounts of the resurrection appearances that follow, and yet remains strangely disconnected from them, for they describe phenomena far more mysterious than the resuscitation of a corpse.

The first resurrection appearance of Jesus is to Mary Magdalene, the same morning as the discovery of the empty tomb. In John's account, she does not initially recognise him.[4] Luke reports an incident the same day in which two unnamed disciples are walking to the village of Emmaus, seven miles outside Jerusalem. Jesus approaches and walks with them, talking about all that has happened and what it all means, based on the Old Testament scriptures. Through all of this they fail to recognise him. He accepts the invitation to stay with them that evening, and as he takes bread, blesses it, and breaks it, finally they recognise him. At that very moment, he disappears from their sight.[5]

Luke and John report that Jesus appeared that same evening to the disciples in Jerusalem. In Luke's account they assume at first that they are seeing a ghost, but Jesus assures them he is flesh and bone like them, and eats with them.[6] John's account specifies that the disciples are in a locked room when Jesus appears, as they are still fearful of the forces that led to the crucifixion of their leader only two days previously.[7] In John's account, the disciple Thomas is absent on this first occasion, and finds that he cannot believe what he is told, but a week later he is locked in with the other disciples in the same place when Jesus appears to them again.[8]

John has the attractive story of a later appearance at the lakeside in Galilee, with Jesus himself preparing breakfast and re-commissioning Saint Peter.[9] Finally in the opening verses of the Acts of the Apostles, Luke writes that Jesus 'presented himself alive by many proofs, appearing to them during forty days, and speaking of the kingdom of God';[10] and in the Gospel and in Acts, Luke explicitly describes a final appearance in which Jesus blesses the disciples and departs from them, being 'lifted up' or 'carried up into the sky'. As they look on, a cloud takes him from their sight, in the episode known as the ascension.[11]

Reflecting on this material, it is virtually certain that the tomb was empty. There may be an entirely natural explanation, but it has never come to light: the phenomenon of the empty tomb remains a mystery. In the resurrection appearances that follow, it seems that the risen Jesus can eat with his companions, show his hands and side, and be greeted without hesitation, but can also remain unrecognised for long periods, enter locked rooms, and appear and disappear at will. These are not accounts attempting to show that the corpse in the tomb was revived. The empty tomb is one phenomenon, and the appearances are another, each pointing separately to the idea that the one they seek is no longer amongst the dead, but is alive again.

Acknowledging that the gospel accounts of the resurrection appearances do not even attempt to describe a resuscitation, we are free to speculate about what they do describe. As a minimum, they testify to a series of profound experiences that the disciples choose to describe in these terms. The women in the garden, having found the tomb empty, nevertheless recognise the presence of Jesus in the cool crisp air of a bright new day. Two disciples walk to Emmaus, talking through all that has happened, and as they break bread, realise that Jesus is with them now as ever, and return to Jerusalem to tell the others of their experience. Gathered there in a locked room, on the day that will become the weekly celebration of the resurrection, the disciples are overwhelmed by the sense that their leader and guide is there amongst them. On the same day a week later, Thomas is also overcome by that sense of Jesus's presence. At the lakeside, Peter finds redemption and a new beginning in a three-fold recommitment following the earlier three-fold denial of Jesus in the hours before the crucifixion. One final experience is recognised as the last in the sequence, and the beginning of a new chapter: tradition has called it the ascension. The accounts become more poetic and dramatic as they are retold. The entire experience may be natural and psychological, and is no less real for that.

It is intellectually lazy to argue that the resurrection appearances took place 'exactly as described', as the account of each appearance begs questions way beyond the descriptions offered. Even if the biblical accounts are taken at face value, the precise nature of the resurrection remains a mystery. Indeed, as a unique event, the resurrection has no precise nature in anything other than self-referential terms, so there is little more that can be said. It is virtually certain that the tomb was empty, and that the disciples experienced resurrection appearances similar to those described. What is absolutely certain is that something significant happened in the days and weeks following the crucifixion, the result of which was the subsequent proclamation of the resurrection of Jesus of Nazareth throughout the region, and then throughout the world.[12]

The Shroud of Turin was an international news item in the early 1980s. It is a long piece of cloth bearing the life-sized image of a crucified man, and is imagined by some to be the burial shroud of Jesus. It has a verifiable history going back to 1357. The image is said to have remarkable almost holographic qualities, and exists only on the very surface of the cloth. Some suggest that it could have been created by a miracle, perhaps at the very moment of the resurrection. As a teenager at the time I was intrigued. I asked my youth fellowship leader for an opinion: whether he 'believed in' the Shroud of Turin. He replied with an immediate confidence that it did not matter whether the shroud was genuine or not: all that mattered was the daily reality of a living saviour. The same logic can be applied to the biblical resurrection stories.

What is absolutely certain is that something significant happened, and is still happening. Two billion people worldwide hold to the religion of the followers of Jesus of Nazareth, and to a creed that declares him alive and declares him to be God. This alone could be called a truly remarkable resurrection.[13] According to the only documents recounting the first origins of the movement, it all began dramatically two days after the crucifixion with events that became known as the resurrection. On this basis alone, we can choose to affirm: 'on the third day he rose again'.

Mary

The resurrection and the return both feature in the original Nicene Creed of AD325. The virgin birth was added only in the Constantinople revision of AD381, when inserted between the two words *sarkothenta* and *enanthropesanta* (became physical and became human) was the phrase *ek pneumatos hagion kai Marias tes parthenou* - from the Holy Spirit and Mary the virgin.

In the section above on the scriptures, the first four chapters of Matthew's gospel were dismissed as preamble. The serious business of the gospel begins with the Sermon on the Mount at the beginning of chapter five. It is perhaps unfortunate that material from the preamble - namely the virgin birth - has made it into the creed, but presumably it was thought important at the time.

The preambles of the gospels record the ministry of John the Baptist, concluding with the baptism of Jesus himself, and a vision of the holy spirit descending upon Jesus like a dove. Jesus then withdraws into the wilderness for forty days alone, before beginning his public ministry and calling his first four disciples.[14]

Matthew, Luke and John have additional preamble material, unique to each of them in turn. John's is the poem of Christ's pre-existence, which presents no practical problems: 'In the beginning was the Word, the Word was with God, and the Word was God; the Word became flesh and dwelt amongst us'.[15] It is Matthew and

Luke who give us infancy narratives: two chapters each.

Matthew's story begins in Bethlehem near Jerusalem in the south, and ends at Nazareth near Galilee in the north, via the visit of the Magi and the flight from Herod's fury into Egypt. Luke's story begins in Nazareth, and records a visit to Bethlehem for a census, the visit of the shepherds, and a story from Jesus's childhood at the age of twelve. Luke also provides an infancy narrative for John the Baptist. It has John the Baptist related to Jesus, and six months older than Jesus. It also has Mary the mother of Jesus present at the birth of John the Baptist: the pregnant Mary goes to visit her relative (*sungenes*) Elizabeth, the mother of John the Baptist, in Elizabeth's third trimester, and stays three months.[16]

In Matthew's account of the conception, Mary is 'betrothed' to Joseph, which, in the culture of the time, may have been an arrangement made between parents when Joseph and Mary were mere children. The shock is that 'before they came together she was found to be with child'. Joseph considers walking away from the arrangement, but is persuaded in a dream to take Mary as his wife as planned, assured that the child is of the holy spirit (*ek pneumatos hagiou*).[17]

Luke's account describes the visit of the angel Gabriel, during which Mary says 'but I have no husband', and the angel explains 'The holy spirit will come upon you, and the power of the most high will overshadow you, therefore the child to be born will be called holy, the Son of God'. Mary then goes to visit Elizabeth for three months. Luke does not record Joseph's reaction to these events, except that Joseph is next seen taking Mary with him to Bethlehem as his betrothed.[18]

The greater mystery in the question of Jesus's parentage is not the emergence of the virgin birth story but the absence of a father. It can be an advantage, for a future guru, to have an honourable father, whether a nobleman or an artisan, or perhaps a dishonourable father, from whom the guru can escape. Outside the preamble material, Jesus appears to have neither. His mother is present repeatedly. She is seen asking Jesus about the shortage of wine at the wedding in Cana of Galilee.[19] She is seen searching for her wayward son, travelling with her other sons but no husband.[20] When Jesus visits his home town, the townsfolk scoff at him: 'Is not this the carpenter, the son of Mary, the brother of James, Joses, Juda and Simon, and are not his sisters here with us?' Joseph is emphatically absent here: 'the carpenter, the son of Joseph' would be a far more natural construction than 'the carpenter, the son of Mary'.[21]

John then places Mary at the foot of the cross on Good Friday. This is highly likely, as she would be in Jerusalem for the Passover festival, but once again the absence of a father is unexplained, and it would be most unusual for a married woman to travel alone.[22] After the crucifixion and resurrection, in the opening verses of the Acts of the Apostles, Mary is seen amongst the group of disciples who 'with one accord devoted themselves to prayer', a group defined as the remaining eleven of the original twelve disciples[23] plus 'the women, and Mary the mother of Jesus, and his brothers'.[24] Joseph is still absent. He is seen in the infancy narratives,[25] then never mentioned again.

The default assumption amongst liberals is that Jesus came from an ordinary large nuclear family: a carpenter father, a home-maker mother, with four named brothers and more than one sister.[26] They will observe that the virgin birth is mentioned only by Matthew and Luke in fanciful and incompatible infancy narratives, and not by Paul or any other early New Testament writer. It is suggested that Matthew was making it all up to match a prophecy in Isaiah, where the difference between a virgin and a young woman (possibly newly married) has become corrupted in ambiguous translation:[27] Luke then incorporates and expands Matthew's idea in his effort to compile a complete record of all existing material.[28]

It is then argued that religious people from New Testament times onwards, including Matthew, have had a problem with sexuality in general, and with female sexuality in particular, so they artificially remove Jesus from any association with sexuality by the story of the virgin birth. The story is then deemed directly harmful, as it subtracts from Jesus's full humanity, and devalues human sexuality. The church later compounds this error by making Mary a perpetual virgin, untouched by husband Joseph and bearing no further children, insisting that all scriptural references to Jesus's brothers and sisters are in fact references to cousins.

This is still the official position of the Roman Catholic church - and the word for brother (*adelphos*) is indeed more flexible than its usual translation implies. In contemporary English, we use the same word 'cousin' in the phrases 'first cousin' and 'distant cousin', even though so-called distant cousins have separate definitions of their own. Most people have heard phrases like 'second cousin' and 'once removed' but few actually know what they mean, and in conversations outside the family would simply say 'cousin'. In the same way, *adelphos* used informally outside the family could mean cousin, a first cousin being for these purposes a 'distant brother' as opposed to a 'first brother', the distinction being less important then than today, as cousins would often live in close proximity and grow up together within a large extended family.

Whether Mary had only one son or a whole group of sons and daughters, there remains the mystery of Joseph's disappearance from the narrative. There are two possibilities. The first is that he was present as a father figure for the birth of Jesus and of any subsequent sons and daughters, then disappeared. The second is that he never existed at all.

The first possibility - that Joseph was present - allows that Joseph may or may not have been the father of Jesus, but leaves his subsequent disappearance unexplained. He is presented in the gospels as an honourable man,[29] so presumably he did not abandon the family, but died. It remains a mystery why such a basic fact should not be recorded, if only by specifying in passing that Mary the mother of Jesus was a widow.[30]

The second possibility - that Joseph never existed at all - takes most seriously the hints of scandal surrounding the birth of Jesus. Joseph's non-existence would account for both the absence of a father figure later in the narrative and the emergence of the myth of the virgin birth. The scandalously pregnant Mary would have been taken in by the extended family - perhaps by one of her own sisters or brothers - and Jesus would have been raised as a brother amongst cousins, hence the ease with which cousins become *adelphoi*. The invention of Joseph on the one hand, and the myth of the virgin birth on the other, are then separate, incompatible attempts to make Jesus's origins less scandalous, which Matthew and Luke then attempt to harmonise in their narratives.

The question that remains is how Mary came to be pregnant. If it was Joseph, the virgin birth myth emerges either as an excuse for Joseph's having pre-empted the transition from betrothed to married, or as a creation of Matthew, followed by Luke, for the entirely negative reasons outlined above.[31] If it was not Joseph, it was either a virgin birth or it was somebody else. Given the culture of the time, it is extraordinarily unlikely that the 'somebody else' option would have been a freely entered, consensual occurrence. It is also unlikely to have been a stranger off the street, and far more likely to have been an older member of the extended family - a process involving coercion and abuse within the extended family. However it came about, Mary would have been taken in by a relative, or taken on by Joseph despite everything[32] – his later disappearance still unexplained.

Mary's visit to her relative (*sungenes*) Elizabeth could now take on a new significance. According to Luke's account, Mary visits Elizabeth in the hill country for three months during the pregnant Mary's first trimester and the elderly Elizabeth's third trimester.[33] Perhaps the story became garbled: it would make more sense for the scandalously pregnant Mary to hide in another village with a relative during her third trimester, keeping her pregnancy a secret and returning home only after the birth. Luke reports that Elizabeth herself hid for five months, and Elizabeth's husband Zechariah kept absolute silence about what was going on inside his home for the entire pregnancy.[34] Perhaps Elizabeth was not pregnant at all, and when the child was born, it was attributed to the elderly Elizabeth and then supposedly adopted by the youthful Mary, producing the other miracle story recorded by Luke, that 'she who was called barren' had finally produced a child in her old age.[35] Mary would then return home with the supposedly adopted child, and settle down to her new life either with Joseph (his later disappearance still unexplained) or as part of the extended family in the home of a brother or sister. Mary left home without a child, and returned home with a child, as in the classic story of the visit to Bethlehem.[36] Back in Elizabeth's village, the story would later spread that Elizabeth's child became a great religious leader later in life. Looking for a way to make sense of this rumour, and assuming that there were two different children involved, Luke would later identify Elizabeth's child as John the Baptist.

If it is unappealing to today's sensibilities to have our human and divine saviour born of a virgin, it challenges all our contemporary prejudices to have him born instead as a consequence of a coercive relationship. It is precisely the kind of challenge the gospel presents repeatedly, as it invites us to value as fully human those on the margins of society: the diseased, the foreigner, the adulterer, the leper, the prostitute, the enemy collaborator.[37] Even the unplanned child, the unwanted child, is loved by God, and a bearer of God's grace. Even the child of a coercive relationship is a child of God, with the potential to become the saviour of the world.

The mother of that child could be a virgin in the Madonna sense. As Christian teenagers in 1984 we piously tut-tutted as Madonna sang 'You make me feel like a virgin, touched for the very first time'. Not many years later we understood the grace and the joy expressed in those words: that whatever she may have been through, a woman can choose to experience herself as unviolated by hideous men and fully healed of past hurts, loved and in love for the first time, 'like a virgin'. It is an empowering image. It can be an empowering image of the mother of Christ: an emotionally robust young woman, choosing to declare herself unviolated, thereby making it true. It is a post-modern tale. And nobody will ever know what really happened, apart from the woman herself. By the time she stands at the cross, her dying son in his early thirties, it was all so long ago.

This final theory is compatible with the strictest reading of both Matthew and Luke - although the disappearance of Joseph remains a mystery. Matthew declares the unborn Jesus to be 'from the Holy Spirit' (*ek pneumatos hagiou*), and specifies that Joseph 'knew her not' until Jesus was born.[38] Luke has the angel Gabriel explaining 'The holy spirit will come upon you, and the power of the most high will overshadow you, therefore the child to be born will be called holy, the Son of God'.[39] Read literally, these are celebrations of the blessedness of the unborn child, not direct or detailed claims about the manner of conception, apart from the specific exclusion - in Matthew's account only - of Joseph.

Having reached a point where this seems the most attractive of the various theories, I find myself choosing not to cling to it. This is not because of what it does to Jesus, whom I would have no difficulty in fully respecting; neither is it because of what it does to Mary, whom I would admire for her resilience and strength of character. I choose not to cling to the theory because it requires the existence of the repulsive individual who did the coercing and the violating. Perhaps I should take this as a challenge in the art of forgiveness. In practice I find it easier not to grant the hideous individual existence in the first place. I find it easier to choose not to cling to the theory.

We have not quite exhausted the liberal opt-outs from the virgin birth. Luke twice refers to Mary and Joseph jointly as the parents (*goneis*) of Jesus.[40] *Parthenos* ('virgin' in the creed), can be ambiguous in Greek, meaning young woman, even young married woman: it can function either side of the wedding day, like our English word 'bride', neatly deleting literal virginity from the literal text of the creed; 'he became flesh from the Holy Sprit and the youthful Mary, and became human'.[41] And literal virginity remains a possibility. Perhaps the elderly Elizabeth had the child, and the youthful and virginal Mary adopted him. Perhaps there was a literal parthenogenesis (birth to a virgin): this is known to science in species as diverse as lizards, turkeys, rabbits and mice;[42] perhaps in a human being it resulted from an intersex or mosaic phenomenon (as described later in the chapter on the seventh sacrament); or perhaps God just willed it to be so, and it was so.

The most intriguing of all scriptural possibilities is a fresh reading of the Melchizedek analogy from the New

Testament letter to the Hebrews. Melchizedek is the first priest (*kohen*) to be mentioned in the Old Testament, and the only acknowledged priest of the Most High (*elyown*) before the giving of the law to Moses. He appears from nowhere in a short passage (just three verses) in the book of Genesis, where he meets with Abraham, then is never mentioned again. All other Hebrew priests in the Old Testament are descendents of Levi, a great-grandson of Abraham. Various myths subsequently grew up around Melchizedek. The letter to the Hebrews quotes them: 'He is without father or mother or genealogy, and has neither beginning of days nor end of life, but is like a son of God, and continues a priest for ever'. Perhaps the writer to the Hebrews is positively celebrating the idea that Jesus's origins are a mystery, and should remain so; that a son of God really ought to appear from nowhere, without father or mother or genealogy, beginning of days or end of life, in order to be an eternal priest, like Melchizedek. If we read the gospel beginning at Matthew chapter five, stripping away the unnecessary preamble, we could be content with exactly that.[43]

The final question is whether to keep Mary in the creed, and if so, how much to say. Protestantism has demonstrated what happens if Mary is deliberately removed from the culture of the faith: its suppression of any hint of devotion to Mary has resulted, in the words of Scott Hahn, in a religion artificially stripped of femininity, and therefore of half its humanity; a religious culture that has the sterile dustiness of a gentleman's club, or the simmering threat of an all-male street gang. Observing that the mother of the king, in Old Testament times, would serve as queen, in preference to any of the king's many wives, Hahn affirms the tradition that has Mary as Queen of Heaven, as well as mother to all who are *en Christo* (in Christ).[44] We do not remove her, but proclaim her: the strong female presence throughout the gospel and the history of the church.

The Holy Family

A close examination of the biblical record may actually give Mary an even more significant role in the gospel project than that afforded her by contemporary Roman Catholicism. A close analysis of the gospel texts reveals a mixed group of both men and women travelling together through the key phases of Jesus's ministry, as it moves from Galilee in the north to Jerusalem in the south. Twelve of the men in the group are named to set up an analogy with the twelve tribes of Israel headed by the twelve sons of Jacob,[45] but the core group of fellow travellers is mixed. Several of the women are named: Mary Magdalene, Joanna, Susanna, Salome, the mother of the disciples James and John, alongside 'the other women who followed him from Galilee'.[46] It is hinted that these independent women with the freedom to travel may even have been bankrolling the entire operation, possibly as wealthy widows.[47]

Both the mother of Jesus and the mother of the disciples James and John are amongst the travelling group, and there may be other kinship relationships amongst the travellers. Several members of the group could be close relatives of Jesus and his mother Mary, including the brothers James and John and their mother, the disciples Jude and the other James, the brothers Simon and Andrew, and Matthew. Far from being a relatively minor figure given undue prominence, Mary the mother of Jesus could be right at the heart of this network.

The brothers James and Jude

There are four lists of the twelve disciples, and they are

fully compatible with each other.[48] The twelve are: Simon who is also called Peter, and Andrew his brother;[49] the brothers James and John (the sons of Zebedee);[50] Philip, Bartholomew, Matthew, Thomas; James 'of Alphaeus', Simon known as the Canaanite or the Zealot, Judas Iscariot, and the other Jude/Juda/Judas, who is 'not Iscariot'.[51]

This latter Jude's unfortunate name is dropped altogether in Matthew and Mark: in Mark he is listed as Thaddaeus, in Matthew he is listed as Lebbaeus.[52] Luke lists him in both the gospel and Acts as Jude 'of James', to differentiate him from Judas Iscariot: it could mean son of James, or it could mean brother of James.[53]

When the townsfolk of Nazareth name the four brothers (*adelphoi*) of Jesus, they include a James and a Jude/Juda/Judas, as well as a Joseph/Joses and a Simon.[54] Amongst the twelve disciples we see two called James, and two called Jude/Juda/Judas. Luke's reference to the Jude who is not Iscariot as Jude 'of James' could make that Jude a brother of James, presumably the James who is not already defined as the brother of John. There is then a James leading the early church in Jerusalem:[55] Saint Paul calls him the brother (*adelphos*) of the Lord;[56] there is also an important apostle called Jude.[57] There are New Testament books ascribed one each to a James and a Jude, with Jude calling himself the brother (*adelphos*) of James.[58]

Now it is possible that these are all different people: that there were countless people called James and Jude involved in the early church, and many pairs of brothers called James and Jude. It is far more likely that at least some of them are the same people. The church traditionally identifies the James and Jude in leadership in the early church (in the Acts of the Apostles) with the two *adelphoi* of Jesus with the same names and with the writers of the two New Testament books bearing the same names. The case for identifying them with the two related disciples of the same names is just as strong in terms of both logic and the scriptural record, making the disciples James and Jude Jesus's *adelphoi*.[59]

The brothers James and John

The names and titles of some of the travelling women reveal further connections.

In John's gospel there are three women named Mary at the foot of the cross: Mary Magdalene, Mary the mother of Jesus, and Mary of Clopas.[60]

Matthew names the group as Mary Magdalene, Mary the mother of James and Joseph/Joses, and the mother of the sons of Zebedee.[61]

Mark names the group as Mary Magdalene, Mary the mother of James and Joseph/Joses, and Salome.[62]

There are various ways of resolving these lists, but the simplest is to observe that Mary the mother of Jesus also has sons called James and Joseph/Joses, making her Mary the mother of James and Joseph/Joses, and placing her, as specified directly in Saint John, at the cross. The circumlocution is the same literary form, associated with humility, that has John using 'the beloved disciple' rather than his own name throughout his gospel. The third Mary becomes Saint Mary Salome of Clopas, mother of James and John, two of the disciples. Mary the mother of James and Joseph/Joses subsequently appears alongside Mary Magdalene in the accounts of both the burial and the visit to the empty tomb, a logical role for Mary the mother of Jesus;[63] Mary the mother of Jesus is then named directly as present amongst the disciples immediately after the ascension.[64]

These three women are all part of the travelling group. Two of them may also be related to each other. An ambiguity in the text of Saint John suggests that Mary of Clopas, the mother of James and John, may be a sister of

Mary the mother of Jesus.[65] This would make James and John cousins of Jesus, and of his *adelphoi* James and Jude.[66]

Matthew, Simon and Andrew

The list of kindred of Jesus amongst the twelve now stands at four, plus two mothers who are sisters, and may rise further.

The James who is not the brother of John is described as 'of Alphaeus',[67] which could be a place name, a brother's name, or a father's name - it is conjecture to translate it as 'son of'. The disciple Matthew is then also called 'of Alphaeus', extending to five the possible number of kinsfolk relationships amongst the twelve.[68]

There is also a Simon named amongst the *adelphoi* of Jesus in Nazareth: it is not impossible that he is also amongst the inner group of disciples, either as Simon Peter or as Simon the Canaanite.

If Simon Peter is an *adelphos* of Jesus, Simon's *adelphos* Andrew is also added to the extended holy family network, bringing the number of disciples who are closely related to Jesus to seven out of twelve (James and Jude, James and John, Matthew of Alphaeus, Simon Peter and Andrew), plus the women.

It now becomes a mark of generous grace that the other five of the twelve (Simon the Canaanite, Philip, Bartholomew, Thomas, and Judas Iscariot), and the other women, are so readily welcomed into this group of kindred, and the seventy-two so readily entrusted with the mission.[69] Right at the heart of this group of relatives and other recruits is Mary the mother of Jesus.

The fatherless family

The absence of a family father figure - whatever its cause - may now be highly significant to the shape of the entire venture. In the first instance it liberates the group - with

Mary at the centre - to engage in such a radical itinerant project. It also adds a powerful poignancy to the presentation of God as the perfect father. The concept may even have emerged and developed through years of conversation within this extended fatherless family group of mothers, sons, cousins, and independent women and men. It also adds poignancy to the words of Jesus that his true kindred are defined not by blood ties but by discipleship, by doing the will of God.[70]

John the Baptist

The final family link is with John the Baptist. If Luke is correct in making Jesus and John the Baptist cousins as well, then the entire gospel project from John the Baptist onwards is a Holy Family project. The public lead is taken first by John the Baptist, and then, after the arrest of John the Baptist, by his cousin Jesus of Nazareth. After Jesus's own forty days of contemplation and soul-searching in John the Baptist's wilderness, Jesus calls his other cousins and brothers to join the project with him. Jesus's scandalously single mother is naturally at the heart of the whole network.[71]

Obsession and Suppression

This conjecture of an extended Holy Family active amongst the disciples cannot be sustained unless we can explain its suppression - albeit not quite its elimination - in scripture and in the centuries since. The clue may be present in two New Testament verses condemning an obsession with genealogies. A section early in the first letter to Timothy describes the gospel aim as 'love that flows from a pure heart, a good conscience, and sincere faith', distractions from which include 'myths and endless genealogies, which promote speculations rather than building up godly faith'. Similarly in the letter to Titus, we read: 'Let those who have believed in God be careful to apply themselves to good deeds, for these are excellent and profitable for everyone, but avoid foolish controversies, genealogies, dissensions, and quarrels over the law, for these are unprofitable and futile'.[72]

We know there were factions in Corinth with rival loyalties to Paul, Apollos and Peter.[73] We also know that Paul had major issues with Peter, but if we look more closely at Paul's account of this in the letter to the Galatians we find that Paul was actually criticising Peter for being influenced by James: Peter was only caught in the middle.[74] On the key point of dispute - legalism and the place of the gentiles - Paul prevailed. Perhaps the last stand of the rival supporters of James was to claim superior authority for James through James's blood-relationship with Jesus, an authority Paul could not claim. This logic could also give authority to Jude, John the Baptist, James and John, Simon Peter and Andrew, Matthew, and all their descendents. This would create the obsession with genealogies (amply demonstrated in the preceding paragraphs here) that the church subsequently suppressed in order to eliminate the vestigial support for James's legalistic party against Paul's anti-legalistic party. This is not Dan Brown's fictional suppression of the bloodline of Jesus, but the actual historic suppression of the bloodline of Mary.[75] The final act of suppression is the declaration by the church of Mary's perpetual virginity: Jesus's brothers and their bloodlines are defined out of existence - every *adelphos* made a cousin, not a brother.[76]

Joseph

Joseph is the only mystery remaining. Perhaps he was invented in a failed attempt to deal with the unmarried parenthood scandal; or perhaps, at the other extreme, he was present throughout, but subsequently eliminated from the text in order to present a virginal Mary and eliminate her bloodline, the bloodline of the brothers of Jesus. The one named brother of Jesus not yet traced is also a Joseph/Joses. If he is the son of the first Joseph, we have two missing Josephs; but perhaps there is only one Joseph, an elder cousin (and hence *adelphos*) of Jesus, in the extended family home that took in the scandalously pregnant Mary: perhaps he became a father-figure to Jesus, also watching over the young Mary, and was wrongly assumed by some to be Jesus's father. Perhaps he stayed at home with the family carpentry business while the others travelled; perhaps he appeared finally at the end of it all as Joseph of Arimathea, who provided the tomb for the burial of Jesus:[77] a wealthy father or cousin in the background all along, or an estranged father doing the right thing at the end, or a father present throughout but otherwise eliminated from the text. The figure remains a mystery.

Mary Unviolate

As for the pregnancy of Mary, we have examined all the possibilities, and none of them - including the virgin birth - is in itself likely rather than unlikely. We can still choose which to contemplate (if any) as part of our devotions, and there is powerful metaphor in the classic notion of Mary Unviolate. Jesus becomes *sarkothenta kai enanthropesanta* - physical and fully human - *ek pneumatos hagion kai Marias tes parthenou* - from the holy spirit and the ever youthful, ever unviolate, Mary the virgin.

I believe in the church

After sections on God as *pater*, on Jesus Christ, and on holy spirit, the revised creed of AD381 concludes with a short miscellany beginning with a declaration of faith in one, holy, universal (*katholiken*) and apostolic church.

We have built the creed around the concept of Yahweh Elohim as infinite compassion and Jesus of Nazareth as its incarnation. The reality is that we have no access to either concept - compassion or its incarnation - except through our fellow human beings. Compassion is understood only in relation to other human beings around us, and our only access to the historic Jesus of Nazareth is through records kept by our fellow human beings. Even our concept of the Christ of faith is built on the idea of humankind and human compassion perfected. Ultimately this faith is dependent on our experience of humankind, and on our hopes and dreams for what humankind could be.

In the creed, we affirm our faith in the human community which is the church: not any single fallible institution, but an undefined essence of church that is holy, universal in the sense of diverse and all-embracing, and linked to a tradition of centuries that goes back to the first apostles. Some have placed the Father in first place in their personal creed, others the Christ, others holy spirit. The reality is that the church, made up of fellow human beings, necessarily comes first. Before we believe in Father, Son or holy spirit, we dare to believe in humankind, in the human community, in the best that humankind can be; in one, holy, catholic and apostolic church. Whatever the order of the text, our personal journey of faith begins not with any version of God, but with an intuitive faith in the potential of humankind. Ultimately we have a humanistic faith, and a humanistic creed.

one holy universal (catholic) and apostolic church.

We have built the case for grasping the concept of Jesus Christ as infinite compassion and Jesus of Nazareth as its incarnation. The reality is that we have no access to either concept of compassion or its incarnation except through our fellow human beings. Compassion is understood only in relation to other human beings around us and our only access to the historic Jesus of Nazareth is through records kept by our fellow human beings. Then our concept of the Christ of faith is built on the idea of human potential and thus compassion perfected. Ultimately the Christ is dependent on our experience of humankind, and on our hopes and dreams for what humankind could be.

In the creed, we affirm our faith in the human community which is the church, not any single fallible institution, but an ideational concept of church that is holy, universal in the sense of inclusive and all embracing, and linked to a tradition of centuries that goes back to the first apostles. Some have replaced God altogether, put Jesus in their place, and others the Christ, others holy spirit. The reality is that the church, made up of fellow human beings, necessarily comes first. Before we believe in Father, Son or holy spirit, we dare to believe in humankind, in the human community, in the best that humankind can be in one holy catholic and apostolic church. Whatever the order of the creed, our personal journey of faith begins not with any custom or creed, but with an implicit faith in the potential of humankind. Ultimately we have a horizontal faith and a humanist creed.

Chapter 5
Prayer

On Miracles

Jesus did not much like doing miracles. He is never seeking to show off or simply prove that he can; far from showing any enthusiasm for the process, he is actually embarrassed by it, and always reluctant. There is always a reason entirely separate from the self-interested desire of the beneficiary.

This pattern emerges in the very first chapter of Saint Mark. Jesus is in the synagogue at Capernaum trying to speak. Somebody is hollering and crying out disruptively like a man possessed. With one word in his direction from Jesus, and one last cry, the man falls silent.[1] Jesus goes from there to the home of two of his disciples, where the mother-in-law of one lies sick with a fever. He takes her hand and the fever is gone.[2] The whole town hears about him and gathers around the door, and he deals with them, but he orders them to tell nobody who he is, and the next morning he is gone long before dawn. The disciples go to find him, saying that everyone is searching for him. This is the point at which he could go back to become a populist miracle-working hero. He goes on instead to the next town, 'that I may preach there also, for that is why I came'. It is the preaching that matters, not the healing.[3]

At the conclusion of the chapter Jesus meets a leper,

rejected and untouchable in the culture of the time, cursed to live outside the city walls in a homeless wandering quarantine, having no contact with the non-leprous population. Moved with pity, Jesus stretches out his hand and touches him: there is always another reason. Jesus now pleads with the healed man, 'See that you say nothing to anyone'. The request is in vain, with the result that Jesus is mobbed whenever he enters a town. He chooses instead to stay out in the country.[4]

We next see Jesus preaching in a private home so crowded that those seeking attention for a paralysed friend lower him through the roof. Jesus's response on seeing him is not to heal, but to free him from any sense of self-blame by declaring the forgiveness of sins. For this he is accused of blasphemy. Speaking angrily to his accusers, he commands the healing as if to prove a point. 'Which is easier to say: your sins are forgiven, or rise up and walk?'[5] There is similar controversy in the next two episodes, as Jesus dines with notorious sinners despite opposition,[6] and breaks the sabbath by plucking grain as he walks through a field.[7] The next healing, at the beginning of chapter three, is a deliberately provocative breaking of the sabbath in full public view in the synagogue.[8] Jesus does not do miracles for their own sake. There is always another reason. Here it is the fundamental controversy over the role of religious law.

In chapter four Jesus calms the storm to save his disciples.[9] In chapter five he heals a wretched man who has been living among the tombs, and sends him home. In the distance a herd of ceremonially unclean swine thunders into the sea.[10] Then in one of the most poignant passages in the whole gospel, we see two stories intertwined. Jesus is called to visit the sick daughter of Jairus, a ruler of the synagogue. On his way there, Jesus is touched by a woman who has had a haemorrhage for twelve years. For this condition she will have been cast out of both temple and synagogue as unclean, effectively by the very ruler of the synagogue to whom Jesus is now attending. In touching Jesus she would have made him ceremonially unclean as well. The ruler of the synagogue and the woman with the haemorrhage represent the opposite extremes of society in terms of the religion and culture of the day. Jesus has compassion for them both. The woman with the haemorrhage initiates the public incident. For the healing of Jairus's daughter, Jesus allows only his disciples and the girl's parents to be present.[11]

In chapter six Jesus feeds the crowd in a deserted place,[12] a deliberate echo of the miraculous feeding of the Hebrew people in the wilderness years,[13] and a first vision of the global eucharist of today.[14] At the end of the day he takes time alone to pray, sending the disciples on ahead into the night by boat. Later he catches up with them on foot, which is practical under the circumstances.[15]

Chapter seven has the healing of the daughter of a gentile woman, identified above as a major turning point in the gospel narrative.[16] A deaf man is taken aside from the crowd for healing in a private place and is asked to tell nobody what has happened.[17] Jesus follows the same process for a blind man in chapter eight,[18] after another great crowd is fed.[19]

The Pharisees now come seeking a miracle for its own sake to test Jesus, and he rebukes them.[20] This is highly significant, showing that the miracles are not there to prove who Jesus is, or anything else about him. It also appears to bring the miracle era to an end, as the mood turns darker in the second half of the gospel story. Only two miracles remain: one to cover the embarrassment of the disciples who fail in an attempted healing in chapter nine,[21] and blind Bartimaeus at the roadside in chapter ten, who cries out to 'Jesus, Son of David', pre-empting the cries of the crowd at Jesus's entry into Jerusalem at the beginning of Holy Week in chapter eleven.[22] Significantly there are no miracles at all in Holy Week itself, apart from the bizarre incident with the fig tree.[23] Miracles are not the essence of the gospel project.

Jesus tells Bartimaeus that he is healed by his own faith: 'your faith has saved you' (*e pistis sou sesoken se*). The same formula is used for the woman with the haemorrhage, and a similar formula in Matthew for the healing of the centurion's servant.[24] Presumably it is also the explanation for the healing of all those who reach out to touch him believing they will receive healing.[25] It is all part of the euphoria of the first half of the gospel narrative, before the mood turns darker. Jesus announces that euphoric era in Luke chapter four - good news for the poor, release for the captives, liberty for the oppressed, sight for the blind[26] - and later in the midst of it all describes it in his message to John the Baptist. 'Go and tell John what you see and hear: the blind receive their sight, the lame walk, lepers are cleansed, the deaf hear, the dead are raised up and the poor have good news preached to them.'[27]

The miracle stories belong to that early era of euphoria. Throughout history and in all cultures, times of spiritual euphoria led by a great teacher or guru are accompanied by stories of miraculous healings and revelations. The distinctive nature of the accounts in the gospels is that there is always another reason: they serve to affirm the humanity of those involved, including the humanity of Jesus himself, rather than blandly showing off his divinity. The message is more important than the miracle.

This principle applies even to the raising of the dead, reported to John the Baptist. The gospels record two incidents: the raising of the son of the widow of Nain in Saint Luke,[28] and the raising of Lazarus in Saint John.[29] In the first of these Jesus is reported to be 'moved by compassion'. The widow has lost her only son and is therefore, in the culture of the time, entirely without support. Jesus raises the son with a touch. The crowds declare that a great prophet has risen up amongst them. Typically for Saint Luke, each detail deliberately compares Jesus to the Old Testament prophet Elijah, who raises up the son of the widow of Zarephath.[30] Lazarus is the brother of Mary and Martha at Bethany, all of whom are close to Jesus. Martha goes to meet Jesus while he is still on his way, and Jesus reassures her only that Lazarus will rise in the general resurrection at the end of time; she returns home consoled. Martha's sister Mary then goes out to meet Jesus, followed by other mourners who assume that she is going to the tomb. She argues with Jesus as she weeps: 'Lord, if you had been here, my brother would not have died'. Jesus is overcome by the emotion of the moment: he is 'deeply moved' at the sight of the mourners, he weeps as he walks with them, at the tomb he is again 'deeply moved within'. Through his own tears he shouts the order for Lazarus to come out.

We can speculate about whether the reported miracles happened exactly as described, but it remains highly significant that those who recorded them did not present them as dramatic public proofs of Jesus's divinity but as illustrations of his teaching, his humanity and his humility. We see a Jesus reluctant, embarrassed by the process, secretive whenever possible, going ahead despite himself when overcome by anger at his adversaries, at injustice, at death itself. The reports appear in the text almost apologetically, always secondary to the humanity of those involved and to the message that celebrates the inherent goodness of their ordinary humanity. When the people come asking for miracles in Mark chapter one, Jesus walks away. When the Pharisees ask in chapter eight, he rebukes them. When he is tempted to summon the miraculous for his own sake, in the temptations in the wilderness at the beginning of his ministry and in the garden of Gethsemane only hours before the crucifixion, his resolution is to remain within the will of God, which is to live a fully human life and death without interventionist privilege.[31]

In the mean time, healing is built into the system. Wounds heal, and increasingly we recognise that health of spirit enriches health of body even as health of body enriches health of spirit. We can also choose to recognise divine benevolence in every positive coincidence: this is the universe - existence and being - in its *abba pater* role. A private serendipity that dispels despair can resonate with a gospel euphoria even today.

On Prayer

As for prayer: it is primarily about relationship, 'the living relationship of the children of God with their Father who is good beyond measure, with his Son Jesus Christ and with the Holy Spirit'. It is 'the habit of being in the presence of God' - a choice embracing the whole of life - within which a specific incidence of prayer or prayerfulness is 'a surge from the heart, a simple look turned toward heaven, a cry of recognition and love, embracing both trial and joy'. It is 'the raising of one's mind and heart to God'. As a final concession, it might even be 'the requesting of good things from God', which is clearly trivial compared to the rest, albeit the most popular.[32] Authentic prayer is about aligning our will with God's will, not seeking to align God's will with ours. The central prayer of Jesus, in which he invites us to share, is 'thy will be done'.[33]

We see Jesus taking time alone to pray. In Mark chapter one he escapes the pressure of the crowd to go out into the countryside alone, long before dawn.[34] We see him praying alone on the mountain all night immediately before choosing the twelve apostles from within the wider group of disciples.[35] In the midst of his ministry, we see him sending his disciples away at the end of a long day and going up into the mountains alone to pray.[36] It is after spending time alone in prayer that Jesus asks his disciples, 'Who do the people say that I am?'[37] - one of the major turning points in the gospel narrative. One week later the Transfiguration takes place when Jesus has taken Peter, James and John with him into the mountains to pray;[38] this prayer may also have gone on all night.[39] Jesus has been praying alone when the disciples ask him to teach them how to pray, and he offers them The Lord's Prayer.[40] And the ultimate representations of Jesus at prayer are those at each end of his earthly ministry: forty days alone in the wilderness at the beginning, and a night of despair alone at the end in the Garden of Gethsemane, as the disciples sleep, in the hours before the crucifixion. On each occasion he is seeking to align his own will with the will of God.[41]

Jesus gives remarkably little direct teaching on prayer, beyond the giving of The Lord's Prayer itself. In the most direct saying, he advises that prayer should be in secret and with minimal words.[42] Even this follows on from the same advice about almsgiving in the preceding verses: a combined warning against the hypocrisy of public piety, rather than direct advice about prayer. Any further advice is gleaned strictly in passing. The injunction that we pray for those who persecute us is more about a change of attitude than specific advice on prayer.[43] Describing future global catastrophes, Jesus does not suggest praying that they do not happen, but only that the effects may be mitigated: 'pray that it may not happen in winter'.[44] In Gethsemane Jesus advises the slumbering disciples to pray that they may not enter into temptation.[45] We have just two glimpses into Jesus's private prayer: he prays for Simon Peter, that his faith may not fail,[46] and he prays for his followers and for those in the future who will come to believe through them.[47]

Twice in parables Jesus assures his listeners that persistence in prayer will be answered, but the invitation is closely defined: the only promise in the parable of the persistent neighbour is that God who is *pater* will give the Holy Spirit to those who ask,[48] and the only promise in the parable of the persistent widow and the unrighteous judge is that God will vindicate in the end.[49] The more confident promise – that if you truly believe and have faith you will receive anything you ask – is mixed in with the bizarre incident of the withered fig tree. Even if we take it as an authentic saying, it remains a strictly limited invitation: presumably those who truly believe will in any case be asking not arbitrarily or selfishly but only in accordance with the will of God.[50] When Jesus directly advises us on how to secure all our earthly needs, he does not mention prayer at all: he advises us not to concern ourselves with such matters, but to seek first God's kingdom and God's righteousness, trusting that all other things will follow on. 'Do not worry about tomorrow: let tomorrow worry about itself'.[51]

Despite all this there is a tradition, even in the mass, of asking for things.[52] There is even a sacrament of anointing with oil for healing, encouraged by an invitation in the letter of Saint James.[53] Anointing for healing is included, along with reconciliation and holy communion, in the so-called Last Rites for the dying, and indeed its use was restricted to this context for many centuries. A prayer for healing – and any true prayer – is ultimately a submission to the perfect will of Yahweh Elohim.

Chapter 6
Community and Sacrament

Community

So far on our tour we have established the concept of Yahweh Elohim, who is Existence or Being, life itself, the ground of all being and the sum of all divinity; we have established an ethic with no list of requirements or prohibitions but instead the invitation to rediscover our own integrity, and through that the fullness of life; and we have recognised a holy book which is a tour of all religions, then an invitation to freedom from both law and licentiousness, living no longer according to the kingdoms of this world but according to the realm of the divine, the kingdom of the air, and the single law of love.

In theory we could take all these riches and meditate on them alone. To do so would be fully in keeping with the direction of contemporary culture, a culture where people live in ever smaller households, manage their own affairs on the basis of a supposed self-sufficiency, carefully guard their privacy and personal interests, and interact with society principally to demand their rights; in short, are almost entirely alone.

This is not what the western tradition commends. Instead, it calls us to gather together. It calls us to community.

'Do not neglect to assemble together, as is the habit of some, but encourage one another.'[1] 'As the body is made up of many parts, so it is with Christ. The eye cannot say to the hand, I do not need you, and the head cannot say to the feet, I do not need you. You are the body of Christ, and each of you a part of it.'[2] 'Those who were baptised devoted themselves to the apostles' teaching and fellowship, to the breaking of bread, and to prayer'.[3]

The custom of gathering creates space in the week to meditate on life and love; an opportunity to contemplate the week past and the week beginning - and our entire situation - in the context of our highest ideals and dreams; and to do all this in the company of others who share our ideals.

Like many who become disillusioned with their church or denomination, or the role (especially the political role) of religion worldwide, I went through a phase of suspecting that all organised religion was necessarily corrupt and corrupting; and yet when understood and maintained in these essential terms - that people of goodwill freely associate together for mutual support as they seek to live by their highest ideals - no harm and only good can come.

Sacrament

And so the community gathers, acknowledging father, son, and holy spirit. It gathers for prayer, and to read the scriptures - making Christ present once again - and to break bread in the ceremony Jesus himself instituted, when he said, 'Do this in remembrance of me'. I cannot guarantee what you will find in your local anglican (Church of England / Episcopalian) or protestant or free church, but in the local Roman Catholic church, in your own town, within a few miles or less, a diverse community gathers weekly, and in smaller numbers daily, for the mass, as here described.

On the night before his crucifixion, at the event which

has become known as The Last Supper, Jesus took bread, gave thanks, broke the bread, and gave it to his disciples, saying 'Take, eat; this is my body, which is given for you; do this in remembrance of me'.[4] Similarly after the meal Jesus took a cup of wine, gave thanks, and said 'Drink this all of you: this cup is the new covenant in my blood,' or even 'this is my blood' – my life-blood.[5]

The mass reproduces the entire sequence, 'in remembrance': the taking, the giving thanks, the breaking of the bread, and the giving of the bread and the cup. Bread and wine are placed upon the altar; the Great Thanksgiving or Eucharistic Prayer is offered, the text varying according to the calendar; the bread is broken; and the bread and the cup are given.[6]

The placing of the bread and the wine upon the altar retains the symbolism of sacrificial offering: self-giving and thanksgiving expressed through the offering of gifts; the offering of the self to Yahweh Elohim, to life itself. These simple gifts of bread and wine will be returned to us as the body and the life-blood of Christ. In the midst of this transaction, they represent the sacrifice of Jesus himself.

The Great Thanksgiving recalls the gifts and works of God – with variations according to the seasons of the church calendar – and makes explicit the connection between the original Last Supper and this event. Recalling the words 'This is my body, this is my blood,' and 'do this in remembrance of me,' it affirms the faith of the church that in every mass the gifts of bread and wine become the body and blood of Christ.

Transubstantiation is a doctrine much maligned. It does not assert any change in the molecules or atoms of the bread and wine, or in their overall appearance to the five senses, which Aquinas calls their form. The term *substance* in this context relates to the Platonic notion that any existing thing has a true essence, a true nature, invisible to our limited senses. This true nature stands behind, or upholds, the form we observe; literally stands under it, as its *sub-stance*. It is this *sub-stance* which changes. The atoms, molecules and form of the bread and wine are unchanged, but their *sub-stance,* their true nature, their invisible essence, become the broken body and poured-out life-blood of Christ, as the community does what Jesus did, and says what Jesus said, in remembrance of him.

In sharing one bread and one cup, the community is united; in the sacramental presence of Christ - as *sub-stance* to the forms of bread and wine - the community is united also with the crucified and risen Christ, who becomes the nourishment, the life-blood, the bread for the journey, both for the community and for each individual within it.

The event as a whole is heavy with imagery. Christ is the host, as at the Last Supper, and also the meal, 'this is my body, this is my blood'. Christ is both the priest, making the offering, and the sacrificial victim who is offered. He is both broken, in the broken bread and the poured-out wine, and alive, as the risen and life-giving one. He is the one remembered, 'do this in remembrance of me', and is also present, in the reading of the gospels, the bread and wine, and the community itself. There is the gathering around one table for a meal - after the example of Jesus himself - and also a holy exchange of gifts: bread and wine exchanged for God himself. The bread and the cup assert the power of the resurrection: pain and death and separation converted into life and beauty and community. The mass, like all the sacraments, represents God made tangibly present in the ordinary elements of our physical world, an ongoing incarnation. The priest declares, 'This is the Lamb of God, who takes away the sins of the world; happy are those who are called to his supper.'[7] The people respond, 'Lord, I am not worthy to receive you, but only say the word, and I shall be healed.'[8]

Baptism - for children or adults - is the mark of membership of this community, with confirmation the independent declaration for those coming of age in a household where they were previously baptised as infants.[9] The sacrament of holy order then sets some apart to serve as deacons, priests and bishops. This is not - or should not be - a declaration of special holiness or privilege: the sacrament of holy order applies to the whole church; it is the way the whole church chooses to organise or order itself.

There are issues about whether the current regime is too hierarchical in its structures, too authoritarian in its exercise of power, unnecessarily discriminatory in its holy order, too sure of itself in its supposed infallibility, too proud in regard to other gatherings of the faithful outside its own structures[10] - but perhaps most significantly for the newcomer it could be more liberal in its sharing of the broken bread. Jesus was content to share his bread with all who would come; the church currently asks for attendance at classes before admitting its own seven-year-olds, or admitting adults through the contemporary Rite of Christian Initiation of Adults (RCIA). A greater generosity in the sharing of the broken bread could revitalise, rather than distract from, the sacraments of baptism and confirmation, which would become more clearly the marks of full membership, the first sacraments of the church's internal holy order: sacraments of commitment, and of the universal call to Christlike ministry.

At the conclusion of the mass, the community is sent out from the gathering to live the life: to live in the world as individuals and as community with the example and teaching of Christ as guide. The catholic dismissal is ever brief: 'Go in the peace of Christ', or 'Go in peace to love and serve the Lord'. This longer free church prayer is based on Romans chapter twelve, and manages to capture the spirit of the positive, practical, humanistic ethic of the Old Testament prophets, John the Baptist, the book of James and the rest of the New Testament, and Jesus himself.

Love with all sincerity. Hate what is evil. Cling to what is good. Be joyful in hope, patient in affliction, faithful in prayer. Bless those who persecute you, bless and do not curse. Rejoice with those who rejoice, and mourn with those who mourn. Live in harmony with one another. Do not repay anyone evil for evil. And the blessing of God – Father, Son, and Holy Spirit – be with you all.

Chapter 7
Eros and the Seventh Sacrament - home life, sex and gender

Welcoming Eros

For that life in the outside world - away from the gathering of the community - compassion is the key to recovering our integrity and experiencing the full potential of life.

This ideal is made practical in the ordinary business of the day: the way we treat our friends, colleagues and neighbours, including strangers and even enemies. Perhaps most intimately and intensely, it is made practical in the way we organise our home lives.

For the vast majority, it is in our home lives that we experience and express love and compassion most intimately and intensely in all their dimensions. There are other ways of living, and other ways of expressing and experiencing love, but for the vast majority the love shared within the home is the most immediate and intense.

The first encyclical of Pope Benedict XVI, published in 2005, is a fifteen-thousand word meditation on the wonder of love and its central place in the Christian tradition. It opens with these words from the first letter of Saint John: 'God is love, and those who abide in love abide in God, and God abides in them'.[1] These words 'express with remarkable clarity the heart of the Christian faith: the Christian image of God, and the resulting image of humankind and its destiny'.[2]

There follows a consideration of 'the vast semantic range of the word love. We speak of love of country, love of one's profession, love between friends, love of work, love between parents and children, love between family members, love of neighbour and love of God' - but one form of love is going to be highlighted as the epitome of all loves for the purposes of this meditation. It is not a specific love within the history of the faith, or within the structures of the church. To quote directly, 'Amid this multiplicity of meanings, one in particular stands out: love between man and woman, where body and soul are inseparably joined and human beings glimpse an apparently irresistible promise of happiness. This would seem to be the very epitome of love; all other kinds of love immediately seem to fade in comparison.'[3]

Western religion has been - and continues to be - unhealthily obsessed with sexuality. The worldwide communion of anglican churches, with historic links to the Church of England, is tearing itself apart over homosexuality. The churches interfere with the legislative processes of national governments almost exclusively where sexuality is involved, concerned with abortion, contraception, reproductive technology, sex education, and any change to marriage or partnership law. In the popular consciousness, the church is obsessed with the sins of others, and by sin means sexuality. *Eros* has been placed in a class of its own, separate from the other loves and in need of special supervision and control. In Benedict's encyclical, *eros* is once again placed in a class of its own, but now as the best of all loves: the epitome of love and the origin of all love both human and divine, not only mysterious and gratuitous like the love of God,[4] but 'rising in ecstasy towards the divine', and 'leading us beyond ourselves'[5] with its 'fascination for the great promise of happiness in drawing near to the other'.[6]

Nothing could better epitomise an incarnational or sacramental faith than the embodiment, the physical expression, of its own highest ideal - and this is what *eros* provides. *Eros* with integrity, uniting body and soul, is the most intense experience of our highest ideal, the greatest human fulfilment and joy. *Eros* without integrity is then the most bewildering and painful of disintegrations, whether experienced as soul without body - as in the classically painful experience of romantic pining - or as body without soul: the body abused and cheapened, the false exaltation of the body turning in a moment to the hatred of the body. In the full flourishing of humankind, 'body and soul are intimately united', experiencing and expressing our highest ideal in harmony.[7]

The Old Testament book The Song of Songs or Song of Solomon is a poetic exchange between two lovers. Early in the text, the word for love is a Hebrew plural, *dodim*. As the song continues, the plural *dodim* is replaced by the singular *ahaba*. This is the progress of *eros*: it begins plural, 'indeterminate and searching', and moves on to 'a real discovery of the other', including concern and care for the other. 'No longer is it self-seeking, a sinking in the intoxication of happiness; instead it seeks the good of the beloved, and it is ready, and even willing, for sacrifice.' The plurality and passion of *dodim* - identified with *eros* - is the energy that necessarily lies behind the emergence of *ahaba*, the prized New Testament Greek concept of *agape* love (pronounced with three syllables, a-ga-pay).[8]

This is the story of godly love. God loves us and cares for us, body and soul. That love is plural, indiscriminate and gratuitous: *dodim* and *eros*. It then becomes focussed on specific individuals and situations: it becomes *agape*. At the same time, infinite resources of new and indeterminate *dodim* and *eros* are available as the energy for the next round of focussed *agape*, and the next one and the next.[9]

The Old Testament account of God's relationship with Israel can be understood in these terms: it is the story of one focussed love within God's wider indiscriminate love for all humankind. The New Testament then bears witness to that universal love, and begins another story of the focussed expression of that love, this time in the followers of Jesus of Nazareth.

Jesus's summary of the law – 'love God and love neighbour'[10] – can also be understood in this way. To love God, the ground of all being and the sum of all that is good, is to offer an unlimited and indiscriminate love. To love the neighbour is to focus that love on specific individuals and situations.

The breadth of our own experience of God can also be understood in this way: in our worshipping communities and in our private prayer we can be caught up, body and soul, in the infinite, eternal and indiscriminate *dodim* and *eros* of God, where we are 'sinking in the intoxication of happiness'; we also experience the *agape* of God's presence in the specific narratives of our own lives and the lives of those around us.

Even the processes of contemporary dating and mating follow this same pattern of development from the general to the specific. The potency of sexual attraction is at first plural, indiscriminate and gratuitous, indeterminate and searching. It is focussed not on any individual but on some imagined ideal, perhaps represented by an unattainable distant individual or type who momentarily represents that ideal. There is even a sense of this powerful experience being shared, in the adolescent years, by fellow teenagers who are lost in the same hormonal fog. This unfocussed *eros* energy has value: it has an appreciation of beauty and potential, and a desire to connect with 'the other'. It is also the raw energy behind the focussed love that may follow. Out of that cloud of unfocussed energy emerge couples who have begun to focus their *eros* energy on each other as specific individuals. By the age of thirty, the vast majority have organised themselves into cohabiting heterosexual pairs. *Eros* has become *agape*: unfocussed *eros* energy has been invested in specific individuals and situations.

Whilst 'the love between man and woman' stands out within 'the vast semantic range of the word love', other intimate human loves can also be understood within the same model, with a transformation from the general to the specific, and embracing both body and soul. From before a child is born until its birth and beyond, parents offer an unfocussed and absolute love for whatever their child may become; as the child grows, that love becomes specific for the particularities of the individual child. Likewise, from birth, the child will reach out indiscriminately to any human form that is a comforting presence, but quickly identifies the mother, then other key carers, as specific individuals within the diversity of humankind: later there is a special place for brothers and sisters, aunts and uncles, cousins, nephews and nieces; for friends, neighbours and colleagues; for spouse and children.[11] This *eros* and *agape* love is fundamental to what it means to be human, present right at the heart of the complex fabric of our lives.[12] It is the single reality of love, emerging with different dimensions appropriate to different situations; it is complete in each case when it gives dignity to both body and soul.[13]

Within the contemporary process of dating and mating, a key moment for an emerging couple is moving in together or setting up home together, which marks the beginning of a status known in contemporary English as 'living together'. The contemporary social consensus is that all emerging couplings up until this moment are temporary trial couplings. These temporary trial couplings now often continue from the teenage years well into the next decade; they are therefore less likely to be known as boyfriend-girlfriend relationships and more likely to be referred to using the more adult and less gender-weighted descriptions whereby two people are said to be 'seeing' or 'going out with' each other, or somebody is said to be 'with' somebody as opposed to being 'single'.

What these couplings have in common - both the temporary trial couplings and the special status of living together - is the universal assumption that they are exclusive. In our contemporary culture people are not expected to be participating in two couplings - even explicitly temporary trial couplings - simultaneously. There may be misunderstandings about when two people are to be deemed to be 'seeing' or 'going out with' each other, or deemed to be no longer 'seeing' or 'with' each other, but the complexities are only around the terms of those definitions: the assumption of exclusivity is universal.

It is less clear at what point contemporary society can safely assume a mutual commitment to permanence in a coupling. This is significant not only for friends and relatives of the couple, but also - more acutely - for the two people themselves. Living together is now regarded as a major statement about intended permanence, as it represents a new level of personal investment in the relationship for each party. In polite society, the 'partner' in such a relationship is cautiously treated as equivalent to a spouse. Despite this, marriage - or formal engagement to be married - is still regarded more comfortably as the point at which permanence can be assumed: the point at which two individuals have consented together to emerge as a permanent couple from the temporary trials of the preceding period. It is the point at which, for these two individuals at least, *eros* is no longer plural, indiscriminate, indeterminate and searching, but focussed within the couple, by each on the other.

The Seventh Sacrament

'Conjugal love involves a totality into which all the elements of the person enter: appeal of the body and instinct, powerful emotion, and aspiration of both the spirit and the will. It aims at a deeply personal unity, a unity that leads beyond the union of the flesh to the union of the heart and soul.'[14]

The western tradition celebrates the possibility of total mutual self-giving as the ultimate expression of *eros*[15] - a self-giving so complete that it includes both permanence and exclusivity.

Mutual consent to this total self-giving is the essence of marriage.[16] If it is absent, impaired or incomplete, there is no marriage, regardless of what may be spoken in any ceremony, recorded in any register, or declared by any authority.[17] If it is present, there is a marriage - registered or not.

The Church of England's 1662 Book of Common Prayer is faithful to this concept. It includes a service not for the creation of holy matrimony but for its solemnisation, that is, its formal public recognition and registration. The phrases 'common law husband' and 'common law wife' were in use well into the 1970s, and the concept still exists in English law exclusively for the purpose of reducing benefit payments to unmarried but cohabiting couples. Common law marriages were entirely equivalent to solemnised marriages in English law until a universally available process of registration was introduced for the first time in 1754. Contemporary moves to give cohabiting couples some of the same rights and responsibilities as married couples represent a return to the situation as it existed before 1754. The ancient common law standard, to resolve the question of whether a couple was married or not, was three occasions of consensual sexual intercourse, presumably on the basis that one or two could be a mistake, but three was a deliberate choice. The standard used in the UK today is cohabitation 'as a couple': the combination of cohabitation and sexual intercourse. A clearer and more dignified echo of ancient marriage ritual is preserved in the common, private and remarkably formal ceremony of proposing and becoming engaged: the groom goes down on one knee, there is a single question with a single answer ('will you marry me'), and the gift of a ring is an optional public declaration of the private exchange.[18]

The intention of procreation is not essential to the sacrament – the church has always recognised the marriages of those who are beyond childbearing age – but the total mutual self-giving that defines the sacrament is assumed specifically to include sexual intercourse, without which the sacrament is deemed incomplete. This requirement is retained in English law even for civil marriages, although both church and state assume that consummation has taken place unless either party to the marriage publicly argues otherwise.

The issue of permanence is probably the most problematic in contemporary society. The sacramental definition of marriage assumes total mutual self-giving, and yet the contemporary consensus may well be permanent provisionality in that self-giving. Divorce is so straightforward and so widely practiced that many will marry with divorce already in mind as an entirely legitimate option, should things not turn out according to their wishes, or should an apparently more attractive situation present itself in due course. A sacramental view of marriage would argue that a marriage according to this consensus is not a marriage at all, as the self-giving at the outset is consciously provisional rather than total. This is not to assert that such a partnership is necessarily harmful or flawed or morally inferior to sacramental marriage if both partners are approaching it on the same basis: it is only to observe that it differs from total mutual self-giving, which defines sacramental marriage, and which might be rather rare.

Half of all registered marriages now end in separation and divorce. The catechism recognises the reality and pain of marriage breakdown: marriage 'has always been threatened by discord, a spirit of domination, infidelity, jealousy, and conflicts that can escalate into hatred and separation'.[19] The church offers two possible interpretations of what has happened. The default assumption is that the marriage was genuine, and is going through a difficult patch: separation may be appropriate, but reconciliation remains the long-term goal.[20] The alternative interpretation is that the marriage was fundamentally flawed at the outset: on the part of at least one of the two parties to the marriage, and possibly both, there never was total self-giving, so there never was a true marriage, despite outward appearances in terms of ceremony and registration. In this latter case, after a due process of discernment, the church will retrospectively declare the earlier supposed marriage ceremony null and void. The two parties to the annulled marriage are effectively declared to be bachelor and spinster again, and as such are free to marry.[21]

Over the last thirty years, mainstream evangelical culture has come to accept the remarriage of divorcees on much the same basis: it tries to say as little as possible on the subject, but if pressed, tends to argue that that the earlier marriage was not a real marriage, being made when the divorced person was young and foolish, or ill-advised, or (ideally) before 'becoming a Christian'; the new marriage is authentic, permanent and indissoluble.

The Eastern Orthodox church takes a different approach, based on the idea that the marriage itself is a living thing. Like any living thing, it can suffer through neglect, and even die. If a marriage is in poor condition through lack of attention, it might be revived - with care and good advice - but if sufficiently neglected for a significant period, it may die. The partners are then free to marry again, more as widower and widow than bachelor and spinster. The English civil courts take essentially the same approach: the marriage was authentic, but is now dissolved; the partners are 'previously married'.

While working as a parish priest, I used to put these two models to any divorced person enquiring about the possibility of a church wedding: was the first marriage flawed at the outset, or was it a true marriage that died? Most immediately recognised which of the two applied to their own situation. In nine cases out of ten it was the western model, that the first marriage was flawed from the outset.

The absence of total mutual self-giving on the public wedding day is not, of course, an invitation to separate regardless of all other circumstances. All relationships start out provisional and conditional. Mutual self-giving within a relationship grows over time. Eventually - without either partner quite recognising when or how - a couple may reach such a point of mutual trust and contentment within their relationship that their mutual self-giving has indeed become total. Equally, total mutual self-giving at the outset does not guarantee effortless permanent contentment for both parties: all relationships need care and attention. The advice of the Old Testament book of Proverbs - relevant to both situations - is 'cling to the wife of your youth'.[22] There is much distress, hurt and harm in the culture of separation and divorce.

The catechism specifies that the parties to an annulled

marriage are free to marry 'provided the natural obligations of the previous union are discharged'.[23] The previous union may not have been a sacramental marriage, but it did nevertheless place moral obligations on both parties which must be appropriately resolved. In the secular courts, 'irreconcilable breakdown' is the classic standard for the granting of a divorce: this is as good a definition as any for the conditions in which separation rather than reconciliation is appropriate, although it does not make the process of discerning such a situation any more straightforward. When such a situation is discerned, less harm is done to the social consensus concerning the permanence of marriage by declaring the previous marriage annulled than by pronouncing a divorce. Taken as a whole, the understanding of marriage defined here positively celebrates the finding of a new love and commitment by the parties to a previously annulled marriage, 'provided the natural obligations of the previous union are discharged'.

Relationships before marriage

Today many temporary trial couplings precede the emergence of stable and married couples from the world of singleness. It is in the nature of these temporary trial couplings that the majority will come to an end. They are usually brought to an end by one of the two partners rather than by spontaneous mutual agreement: it is the process known by the other partner as being ditched or dumped, or otherwise smoothed over by many euphemisms, but nevertheless painful, certainly for one partner and often for both. How painful the separation will be is dependent upon how far the relationship has progressed. Breaking up after two or three evenings out is very different from breaking up six months or a year into a relationship, and different again from breaking up after moving in together, or becoming engaged, or marrying.

Some have sought to deny that the hurt exists, but the reality is that it does exist, somewhere on the scale between disappointment and bereavement.[24] The degree of hurt is dependent not so much on the length of time the two people have known each other as on how much each has invested in the relationship. That investment will have encompassed 'body and instinct, powerful emotion, and aspiration of both the spirit and the will'.[25] All of these are hurt when the relationship comes to an end.

Avoiding hurt is right at the heart of our ethical system, so avoiding or limiting the hurt of breaking up becomes a moral imperative. Historically some highly structured societies have attempted to achieve this by banning this phase of trial couplings, but such a draconian curtailment of personal freedom is unlikely to add to human wellbeing overall. A sequence of trial couplings allows people to look for a compatible partner, which sounds brutal, but the reality is that for the level of intimacy that *eros* seeks, within a diverse human race, some potential partners are more readily compatible with each other than others.[26] Ultimately this can only be discerned by the individuals themselves, hence the practical necessity of temporary trial couplings on the way towards the emergence of permanent committed pairs. Some hope to find a relationship with someone so compatible that the relationship can be totally fulfilling in return for zero effort, but of course no such relationship exists. Nevertheless, in any appropriate coupling, the returns for both parties are far greater than either's investment. Such is the simple logic of the companionable sharing of two lives, and the ultimate goal of *eros*.

Still there remains the problem of the hurt of breaking up in the necessary trial phase. It cannot be avoided.

Perhaps at least it can be limited. This means limiting, or at least being aware of, the level of investment - the investment each party is making in the relationship, which will be lost if the relationship ends. The simple advice is not to invest too much too soon. Unfortunately if *eros* is ever to progress, if couples are ever to emerge at all, something has to be invested, risks have to be taken, there has to be self-giving, but it is wise to be aware just how much, and just how soon. The ritual of marriage, whatever it may mean today, was originally intended to mark the point at which a couple finally agree together to invest everything.

The Falling Age of Puberty

A dramatic contemporary phenomenon - relevant to our consideration of *eros* - is the continuing fall in the average age of puberty. With improvements in general health and nutrition, the average age of puberty has been falling consistently by about four months per decade for the last one hundred and fifty years: by four and a half years already, and still falling. Young people are experiencing the hormonally supercharged *eros* of puberty earlier and earlier.

Professors Mark Hanson and Peter Gluckman believe that the age of puberty is actually reverting to its natural level, having been driven artificially high by the disease, poor health and poor nutrition of agrarian and feudal living and early mass urbanisation, compared to the hunter-gatherer conditions in which the human species evolved. They speculate that in such ancient societies, a young person reaching puberty at the same age as today would already have attained 'the degree of psychosocial maturation necessary to function as an adult'. As human society became more complex, poorer health and nutrition artificially delayed puberty long enough for young people to complete the increased level of education necessary to function as adults in those increasingly complex cultures. This all changed in the twentieth century, as improved health and nutrition saw the age of puberty fall again, while our vastly more complex society routinely began to keep young people in full time education until the age of eighteen or twentyone or beyond. Their conclusion is that for the first time in our 200,000 year history as a species, young people are becoming sexually mature before becoming psychologically equipped to function as adults in society.[27]

The gap between puberty and full time work is the period we call adolescence, and it is indeed an entirely new phenomenon, first emerging during the twentieth century, and now dominating each individual's entire second decade. It is not necessary, however, to equate the degree of social maturity required to cope well with puberty with the level of general education required for economic success. If young people are reaching the age of puberty ill-equipped for its hormonally driven emotional charge, it is not because the economy has become more complex requiring more years in education, it is because we have failed to encourage their social development: Hanson and Gluckman themselves assert that 'the degree of psychosocial maturation necessary to function as an adult' can be achieved by the current age of puberty, and indeed was achieved by that age in simpler societies. For the sake of economic success, young people today may need to remain in education until they are eighteen or twentyone, but this is not the cause of any delay in social maturity.

If there is such a delay today compared to primitive societies - and I suspect that there is - its causes lie elsewhere in the structure of contemporary society, both inside and outside the home. Children today are delayed in learning the social skills required for adult life because conversation and social interaction between generations - and even between age groups - have virtually disappeared. The dining table - once the meeting place of the generations and of all age groups - has disappeared from most homes, replaced by the television or televisions, in ever smaller households; and socialisation away from the home is strictly by age group, a pattern encouraged by the education system, which separates the entire population into social groups strictly by date of birth. In the African proverb it takes a village to raise a child. Today's child is offered the television and a room full of children exactly the same age as themselves. Given instead a home life and a social life where generations and age-groups communicate and interact, there is no reason why a modern child should not be fully equipped to cope with puberty by the time it arrives.

My goddaughter is a talkative and inquisitive five year old. Every evening one of her parents will sit down with her and ask her to describe the best moment and the worst moment of the day just ending, and reciprocate with their own. It is top quality family time: it keeps lines of communication open, and as a daily routine it is standing them all in good stead for the years ahead. As a matter of principle her parents always answer questions honestly. It is encouraging a confident, inquisitive and talkative daughter. On her last visit she enjoyed telling me where children come from: Mummy and Daddy go to bed together and make kissy-kissy love, then the baby grows inside Mummy's tummy, and then - this last part delivered with wide-eyed shock - the baby comes out of Mummy's bottom. Later she set about describing every family home she could remember. Each one was headed by a couple. She would name each partner, describing one as 'the boy' and the other as 'the girl'. She would add the names of the children, and then explain what names or titles they used to address each other. This mostly involved repeating that the children called their own parents Mummy and Daddy, which seemed superfluous, until she described in great detail and with remarkable sensitivity a family where there are two natural children and three foster children, and another where there had been a divorce and at least one remarriage. Finally she picked up on a subject that she felt her mother had not explained sufficiently, namely why my partner and I, who were clearly analogous to any other married couple, were not in fact married. Her mother had assured her that my partner and I surely love each other very much, but could not get married because we were both boys. This was clearly an unsatisfactory answer, so she asked me instead. As it was only weeks since we had taken advantage of the new civil partnership legislation, it seemed churlish not to explain that 'this new thing had come in' that was like marriage, but for two boys or two girls. Delighted, she ran off to tell Mummy. Later Mummy rolled her eyes and assured me that the entire school class would know all about it by the end of Monday morning.

There is no reason why a five year old should not know all these things. Indeed, with girls routinely starting their periods as young as nine or eight or seven, there is every reason why they should. 'Psychosocial maturation' does not need to be delayed just because full time education now continues to the age of twentyone, and top quality sex-and-relationships education should be on the school curriculum long before puberty, with the basics completed before the end of primary school. It could all begin at the age of five, with the story of kissy-kissy love.

Some fear that such openness and education will corrupt children, or make them experiment. I do not regard my goddaughter as in any way corrupted – on the contrary much damage is done by secrecy - and all the international evidence is that openness and top quality sex education not only reduce rates of teenage pregnancy and sexually transmitted disease, but actually increase, rather than decrease, the age of first intercourse. By the same token, in an age that is greatly concerned about paedophilia, it is far easier for a child to resist coercion if he or she actually understands what is being suggested, and has learned, as a matter of principle, that throughout life he or she will have the absolute right to say no. It is entirely possible for children to be prepared for puberty well in advance, and all the evidence - unsurprisingly on reflection - is that empowerment by knowledge and by relevant social skills helps them to handle the experience more positively, and to enjoy an adolescence with better emotional and physical health.

Advice for the Adolescent Body and Soul

It is worth considering what direct advice can legitimately be offered to adolescents as they try to negotiate this novel ten year period of their lives - in addition to factual education and basic social skills - if only because so many others are rushing to offer advice.

The defining characteristic of adolescence is an overwhelming experience of *eros*.

Morally we have established that *eros* is a gift, the greatest of gifts, giving dignity to both body and soul. It is not only pointless to attempt to suppress it, but morally wrong.

We have also established its practical dimensions: it moves from the plural and indiscriminate to the focussed and particular; it emerges with different dimensions appropriate to different situations; eventually in one situation it may bond with the other in total mutual self-giving.

The key to making moral sense of the intense adolescent experience of *eros* lies at the point where the moral and the practical analyses meet: in the recognition that in its fullness *eros* embraces both body and soul, and if there is to be integrity rather than disintegration, every expression of *eros* - every relationship - should embrace both body and soul.

Eros does this naturally. Every human relationship has a physical expression, indeed it is only through our bodies that we relate to each other at all. It begins with the body language of how we stand or sit: how close, and how formal. It moves on, as and when appropriate, to a touch, a handshake, a warm embrace. Every relationship from the supermarket checkout to the workplace, from a social event to the marital home, has its appropriate physical expression - partly defined by culture, mostly innate. Contentment within each of these diverse relationships is dependent upon its appropriate physical expression. The intrusion of an inappropriate physical expression can cause both hurt and confusion - as can the artificial absence of an appropriate one.

There is no specific dividing line between this universal physical relating and the sexual. In a particular relationship of special intimacy and intensity, the physical relating moves onwards from a touch, a handshake and a warm embrace towards tenderness, nakedness, and sex. There is a continuum - embracing both body and soul - from the most fleeting acquaintanceship to the most intimate lifelong partnership, as *eros* emerges with its different dimensions appropriate to each situation. It goes wrong when body and soul get out of sync.

The best approach is not to lay down puritanical and censorious legalistic rules but to trust the nature of healthy *eros* and basic social skills. Healthy *eros* - with integrity rather than disintegration - will instinctively keep relationships of body and soul in balance, and will know when that balance has been lost. As for basic social skills, most of what teenagers need to know they will know by the age of seven if lines of communication have been kept open; things like 'some friends only want to know you for what they can get out of you', which in this context gently reinforces the idea that genital intimacy is something valuable and desirable, not something cheap or dirty or wrong. And so the first piece of advice would be 'let it come naturally' - the holding of hands, the kissing, the intimate touch. 'Let it come naturally' includes both 'don't be pushy' and 'don't be pushed', and beyond that invites body and soul to move forward together or not at all, as they naturally and healthily would.

The second piece of advice would be to 'remember that splitting up hurts - and the more that you've done, the more it will hurt'. To enter into a relationship is not only to discover and build a wonderful shared happiness now, it is also to risk hurt to both parties later. To enter more intimately, more intensely, for greater time, multiplies happiness now, but also multiplies the risk of later hurt. The challenge is to take account of that risk of hurt, alongside the intoxicating, mutual, God-given joys which are the promise of intimacy of body and soul. Perhaps there are some levels of intimacy so incredibly painful to break that it is worth holding back from them until each partner can promise the other that the relationship will never end, and can trust that promise. The Church's traditional teaching is that this level of intimacy - in an appropriate balance of body and soul - is defined by such things as setting up home together, sharing all worldly goods, and having sex; and that the associated promises should include the promise to stay together through the good times and the bad 'until death us do part', whatever the future may bring.

Of course the sex is the most controversial part of this definition. This is not a problem for the church alone: the attitude of society at large also swings between extremes. In the 1960s, sexuality was celebrated: it was even believed that its pleasures might be separated out not only from the processes of pregnancy and childbirth but from the complex and demanding business of commitment, affection, and any kind of ongoing relationship. In the 1970s, the most extreme radical feminism began to redefine all heterosexual intercourse as rape: heterosexual intercourse became the ultimate icon of all male abuse and domination of women, to which no self-respecting woman would voluntarily submit. Today the extremes of attitude are age-related, with society assuming that sex is so healthy as to be virtually compulsory for the over-thirties, but so corrupting as to be necessarily forbidden by law for anyone under the age of sixteen.

These extremes represent the two sides of the reality of the human experience of sex. There is good sex and there is bad sex. The difference between the two is highly geared. Good sex is one of the highest pleasures of human experience, perhaps the highest. Bad sex is said to be one of the most destructive influences possible in any human life: violating and soul-destroying. There are pleasures in sexuality to be celebrated; there are also cautionary tales to be told.

It is not that we want adolescents not to have sex: it is that we want them to have the best possible lives, making wise choices. It is better to equip them for that task with information, accumulated wisdom and social skills, than to disempower and depress them - and earn their contempt - by imposing arbitrary laws, or being persistently negative about what is potentially one of life's greatest joys.

Parts of teenage culture are so aggressively pro-sex

that sex seems virtually compulsory: inescapable in any heterosexual friendship, and a matter of public shame to be without. In 2005 two church-based youth workers in north London organised a unique social and cultural experiment called the Romance Academy. They were to take a mixed group of a dozen sexually active young teenagers and challenge them to manage without sex for five months. The group would meet weekly for discussion and peer support. The youth workers hoped to demonstrate that sex could get in the way: that too much sex too soon could damage, rather than enhance, any relationship. What happened over the ensuing months was beyond anything they had imagined. The teenagers developed self-esteem. They came to respect themselves and their bodies. They realised - boys and girls alike - that they were giving themselves away too soon, in the desperate and vain hope that they might be loved as a result. What they discovered in their celibate months was that they were worth more than that, and could aim for so much more: that there is more to life than sex, even for a teenager. 'You start looking at the opposite sex as a person, not an object.' 'You go out looking for friends, not for sex.' 'I feel special now, I have more dignity.' 'A lot of teenagers agree to sex because they can't think of a reason to say no.'[28]

Age of Consent

The current age of consent in the UK actively discourages the kind of conversations made possible by the Romance Academy. The age of consent was raised to the current sixteen as recently as 1956. Until 1956 it had been thirteen, since 1875; before that ten, since 1576. The age of consent is at a historic high at a time when the age of puberty is at an all time low. In the international context, with the exception only of the Republic of Ireland, the UK currently has the highest age of consent in Europe - and the highest rate of teenage pregnancy, some of the highest rates of teenage promiscuity and sexually transmitted infections, and one of the lowest average ages of first intercourse.[29] The Sexual Offences Act 2003 goes further than any previous law by criminalising the ambiguously defined act of sexual touching between under-sixteens, which almost certainly includes kissing and hugging between boyfriend and girlfriend: consent is deemed impossible, and the specified term of imprisonment is five years.[30]

Presumably the intention behind the law is to enhance the well-being of younger adolescents. It is almost certainly counter-productive. By criminalising their behaviour, the current law makes it far more difficult for adolescents to seek advice, whether medical, legal or emotional. At the simplest level, they are dissuaded from asking any adult for basic relationship advice. If they do seek advice, the conversation is likely to focus on the legal situation rather than the particular relationship in which the adolescent is engaged, leaving the adolescent without the very advice that he or she is seeking. Adolescents are also dissuaded by the law from seeking the best medical advice, and in the event that an adolescent does suffer abuse, he or she is dissuaded from reporting it, as their previous consensual sex will have been just as illegal as the abuse.

At the more conceptual level, we have actually criminalised the healthy development of *eros*. The sheer power of adolescent *eros* will ensure that if its healthy expression is suppressed, unhealthy expressions will emerge instead. Our primary concern is not delaying sex - for which the law has failed in any case - but encouraging the healthy development of *eros*, the greatest of human gifts and a glimpse of the divine, giving dignity to both body and soul. What this requires is not the criminalisation of young people, but their empowerment with the knowledge and social skills appropriate and necessary to their physical development. The international evidence is that this empowerment reduces promiscuity, increases the average age of first intercourse, and improves both mental and physical health. These are the natural consequences of the healthy development of *eros*, as opposed to its suppression and criminalisation.

The key to decriminalising adolescent *eros* is the inescapable logic of harmonising the age of criminal responsibility and the age of consent. If a young person is deemed mature enough to give intelligent informed consent to something as socially complex as criminality, that same young person is surely mature enough to give intelligent informed consent to physical intimacy. Equally, if a young person is deemed incapable of giving intelligent informed consent to physical intimacy, that same young person is surely incapable of giving intelligent informed consent to something as socially complex as criminality. The best protection for young people is not in their universal criminalisation, but in knowledge and social maturity, in the encouragement of healthy rather than unhealthy *eros*, and in the universal principle of consent. The age of criminal responsibility is currently eight in Scotland, and ten in England and Wales.[31] These are the lowest ages in Europe, creating by far the longest period of universal adolescent criminalisation.

Pro-marriage

Christianity has been caricatured as being opposed to sex before marriage – a pointless opposition to a virtually universal phenomenon. Worse than this, the churches have largely surrendered to this caricature, albeit often with some embarrassment. The tragedy is that this negativity is not a faithful interpretation of the tradition, but involves a confusion of terminologies and anachronisms.

Before the reformation era the church showed little interest in registering marriages, taking the common law approach in which sex effectively was marriage, rendering the phrase 'sex before marriage' meaningless. A more legitimate reading of the tradition is not negative but positive: not negative about sex, but positive about commitment, faithfulness, stability, and ultimately total mutual self-giving – for the advancement of human integrity in harmony of body and soul.

The promotion of this positive agenda does involve advising against those practices that detract from it, such as reckless and promiscuous sex, adultery, and the marriage breakdown that leads to divorce. In practice – rather than as a purely philosophical exercise – there are not many who would promote reckless or promiscuous sex or adultery or marriage breakdown as projects likely to enhance human wellbeing when contrasted with commitment, faithfulness, stability, and mutual self-giving; and yet a striking phenomenon of the last three decades is an increasing reluctance to make commitments: as we enter the new century, the average age of first marriage is at a historic high, and still rising.

For all the talk of free love during the 1960s, the average age of first marriage actually fell during that decade, and remained low in the early 1970s. Since then, it has risen inexorably at an unprecedented rate. It has now passed 30 with no sign of slowing down. The new population of adolescents, itself a phenomenon of the last fifty years, is growing into an equally unprecedented population of unmarried young adults in their mid- and late-twenties. The gap between puberty and the commitment of marriage – once negligible – is now rapidly approaching two decades, and continues to expand.

This nervousness about commitment is understandable, with half of all marriages ending in divorce, and half of all cohabitation relationships breaking down within two years. The church would do well to rise above its caricature image of censoriousness about sex, and focus instead on actively encouraging commitment, faithfulness, stability, and ultimately total mutual self-giving. The church could actively promote these as the ultimate expression and experience of *eros*, leading to a conjugal love 'that leads beyond the union of the flesh to the union of the heart and soul'.[32]

Gay Life

In our exploration of *eros* and mutual self-giving, no roles or commitments have been assigned according to gender. The arrangement is wholly symmetrical. It works without concern for the gender of either party in the emerging couple. The catechism speaks doggedly of the spouses, in preference to husband and wife or bride and groom.[33]

This becomes significant when considering the possibility that the two equal partners might be of the same gender. If the role and status of each partner is the same, the gender of each partner is irrelevant. If a couple emerges from the fog of adolescent *eros* as a same-gender couple, in total mutual self-giving, that couple falls within the essential sacramental definition of marriage. To insist at this point that difference - specifically difference of gender - is essential to the sacrament is to introduce a concept of two different roles within marriage which, in the discussion so far, has been entirely absent. By adopting a model for marriage which is essentially a union of two human beings as equals, the 1992 catechism, and society at large, leave no logical grounds for the exclusion of same-gender couples.

For the vast majority of individuals, a strong early sense of discrimination emerges within indiscriminate *eros* - long before any focus on a specific individual - favouring conjugal intimacy with one gender rather than the other. For many, this discrimination favours a same-gender partner. In my own generation it seemed terribly important to try to justify this, with historic precedents and scientific explanations. A new generation is entirely content to accept that homosexuality simply exists, and is morally no different from - and no more mystifying than - the majority experience of heterosexuality. It needs no justification: it is what it is, and its expression is morally no different from the expression of heterosexuality.

During decades of criminalisation, and centuries of social disapproval, homosexual *eros* often took less wholesome forms than heterosexual *eros,* as suppressed *eros* will. With decriminalisation and increasing social acceptance, homosexual *eros* emerges in exactly the same form as healthy heterosexual *eros*: far from conforming to an earlier promiscuous and irresponsible stereotype, people with homosexual *eros* are choosing to form permanent, faithful, stable relationships analogous to marriage, and are demanding that state and society recognise them as such. Since December 2005, with the civil partnerships legislation, both the state and the social consensus have done precisely that.[34]

This new social consensus includes the church, at least away from the hierarchy. The relevant theology has been around for decades, all with origins confidently within the western tradition. The supposed biblical case against homosexuality depends entirely on the misuse, and the wanton mistranslation, of a handful of obscure biblical texts.[35] All that remains beyond that is the hierarchy's self-referential impulse towards the justification of its own past prejudices.

LGBT

By the late 1980s, the politics of homosexuality was understood as a branch of anti-sexism, on the basis that gender is irrelevant. The exception was amongst a certain sector of lesbian separatists, who saw lesbianism as the practical outworking of feminism, and were openly misandrous (hateful towards males). The clashes caused by this difference of approach within gay organisations - universally renamed Lesbian and Gay on the back of 1970s feminism - were not edifying, but only ten years previously many homosexual men had understood their own homosexuality as one part misogyny to one part acknowledging the feminine within, a feminine side rendered acceptable, in its misogynistic way, by not actually being female.

The true exemplars of the new anti-sexist political consensus were of course bisexuals, the only minority actually operating in accordance with the central hypothesis that gender is irrelevant. Lesbian and Gay politics was renamed once again, briefly as LesBiGay, then universally by the acronym LGB, although few organisations actually changed their name again. In practice, most gay people were deeply suspicious of bisexuals, assuming that they would always be unfaithful, and would ultimately desert their same-sex partners for the social convenience of marriage. In reality there is no more reason why a bisexual person should be unfaithful than a 'monosexual' person, who in theory could be attracted to half the human race. The concept of bisexuality may actually embody a certain honesty about the initially indiscriminate, gratuitous and plural nature of *eros*.

The anti-sexist LGB alliance was next challenged by a group for whom gender was anything but irrelevant. Transgendered people experience a direct mismatch between their internal sense of their own gender and their apparent physical gender. Their issues are less about to whom they feel drawn, and more about who they understand themselves to be in relation to others; not about what they seek, but about who they are, and therefore what they can offer in any relationship. Transgender politics insists that this is not a choice or preference, but is part of their fundamental and inescapable experience of self. As with male and female homosexuality, the experience seems to be fixed early in life, and while various physical or psychological causes have been suggested, none has been found.

Transgendered people may have represented an even greater challenge to the LGB alliance than to the mainstream heterosexual population. There is a suspicion about the transgendered person's desire for surgery or medication to alter the body: it smacks of self-mutilation, which is often a response to self-hatred, and self-hatred is what many gay people have overcome by a change of attitude, not by surgery or drugs. There is also a feminist objection to the idea of men masquerading as women, or of women abandoning the feminist cause to join the ranks of the enemy. Most significantly, the transgender experience refuses absolutely to entertain the premise that gender is meaningless or irrelevant. It opens up instead an entirely new debate about what we mean by gender. With this last question in particular left unresolved, the transgender cause has nevertheless been accepted by the existing informal alliance of minority interests, and the universal acronym of sexuality and gender polity is now LGBT. In the UK, under the terms of the Gender Recognition Act 2004, transgendered people can now apply for a new birth certificate in their new name and newly 'recognised' gender, providing them with a legitimised and effectively anonymised history, and with the right to marry (or form a civil partnership) according to the gender in which they have resolved to live.

Intersex

With each letter now representing a closely-defined category of persons, the definitions implicit in the list LGBT can begin to look strangely exclusive. Some organisations add A for allies or S for straight, but the exclusivity of the four LGBT definitions remains. The more inclusive proposal is to replace the entire list with Q for queer, representing the all-embracing diversity that gay originally represented. It blurs all boundaries, and invites everyone to consider just how monochrome or diverse their own experience of *eros* might be. In practice Q is more commonly added to the end of the list, for queer or for questioning - a welcome to the undecided that leaves the other categories intact. Far more interesting for our purposes is the addition instead of the letter I, representing the emergence from the shadows of the physical, medical and biological phenomenon of intersex.

As much as one percent of the population defies simple categorisation as either XX-female or XY-male at the entirely physical level, before any conversation about sexual orientation or gender identity. There are chromosome collections other than XX and XY,[36] there are mismatches between the chromosomes and the genitals, and there are ambiguous genitals, where the pre-natal adaptation of the initially gender-neutral genitals has not completed its usual course of development into genitals unambiguously either male or female.[37]

Androgen Insensitivity Syndrome is an example of an intersex phenomenon unrecognised before modern medicine. In AIS, a chromosomally male (XY) individual is insensitive to the action of the male hormone androgen, the hormone which would normally lead the body to develop male sexual characteristics. By external appearances the individual is entirely female. For most of history, AIS individuals were simply infertile females. In the late twentieth century, blood chromosome tests were introduced to establish that female athletes were authentically female. A Spanish female athlete who turned out to be an XY individual with AIS was stripped of her medals. On appeal, her medals were reinstated. International athletics now has no agreed definition of female.[38]

Forms of intersex which produce ambiguous genitalia at birth have been known throughout history. Any prenatal variation in the usual pattern of exposure to various hormones - or of sensitivity to those hormones - can result in ambiguous genitalia. In the west as many as one in five hundred births have genitalia sufficiently ambiguous to be referred for surgical intervention, in order that they might be altered to resemble more closely those of one gender and not the other. The default option is to aim for female, on the basis that it is supposedly simpler to construct surgically. Intersex campaigners resent this surgical intervention, which they regard as an entirely inappropriate way to deal with a problem which is actually the parents' and society's, not the child's. Other aspects of intersex ambiguity emerge at puberty when the development of secondary sexual characteristics and standard male or female sexual function can be disrupted by any variation in the usual pattern of production of hormones or sensitivity to those hormones, or the action of any of the fifty-four other genes identified so far that coordinate various responses to the presence of either XX or XY.

Whilst arguing against any surgical intervention, intersex campaigners do recommend the assignment of intersex children to one gender or the other, but only because society continues to be organised on the basis of such assumptions. They recommend the giving of a name which the child can retain if he or she chooses to switch gender role later, an option that should be considered repeatedly throughout childhood: a holiday presents an opportunity to try on a different role, a change of school an opportunity to make a more permanent change. In adulthood, many intersex individuals are delighted to throw off the shackles of their assigned gender role, but differentiate their experience from that of the transgendered: they are not leaving one gender role in order to join another, but leaving an arbitrarily assigned gender role in order to live as intersex. A series of public awareness posters reads, 'I am not a man or a woman, I am both.'[39]

The transgendered make us question what we mean by gender, in their strong desire to leave one publicly recognised gender role and join the other. Feminism, anti-sexism and the LGB alliance also challenge the conventional categories in various ways. The existence of intersex confirms that gender is not a straightforward binary phenomenon: in the biological sphere as well as the social, there is a continuous scale of gender from male to female. Most gather in one of two clusters, in a bimodal distribution. The transgendered feel strongly that they are stuck in the wrong cluster, but we all play games with both biological and social constructs of gender: men can be carers, women can go to war; fashions in hair and clothing pass from one gender to the other; most men shave, feminising their appearance; many women augment their height with raised heels and padded shoulders, and slim down and tone up towards a masculine body shape. We find ourselves slightly suspicious of those who are too extreme in their masculine or feminine role; and to demonstrate that the variations are multidimensional, most homosexual people are entirely content with their own gender.

Mosaicism

Perhaps the most intriguing form of intersex is that resulting from the phenomenon of mosaicism. The origin of mosaicism is the early fusion of two embryos which would otherwise have become fraternal (non-identical) twins. This happens early in the process of embryo development, before cell differentiation has begun: it is the opposite of the phenomenon of early embryo division that produces healthy identical twins. The result is a single healthy individual who contains two fraternal sets of DNA. Each cell or organ contains only one set of DNA, but viewed as a whole the body is a mosaic of cells and organs containing two distinct sets of fraternal DNA.

The phenomenon of mosaicism has only come to light through the contemporary science of detailed DNA testing. Only thirty cases have been formally documented worldwide. Amongst them is the case of a woman who, according to initial DNA testing, was the aunt, not the mother, of some of her own children. Further testing revealed that she was a mosaic of two fraternal sets of female DNA: some of her children were descended from one set, and some from the other. In another case, a young male patient was examined after being referred for an undescended left testicle. The examination revealed, on the left side, an ovary and a fallopian tube. The patient was a mosaic of male and female DNA.

Mosaicism may be far more common than we imagine. Most mosaic individuals show only the most subtle signs, such as mismatched eyes or parti-coloured hair, or may show no signs at all unless extensively tested in different parts of the body for DNA. Without this extensive testing, there is no way of knowing how many individuals are harbouring undetected mosaicism.

There is also a known phenomenon of micro-mosaicism. About eight percent of fraternal twins are blood-mosaic of each other: in their blood they each have significant quantities of the other's DNA. Some singletons are also blood-mosaic, presumably from a non-surviving fraternal embryo twin. This mosaicism in twins could be a result of embryo fusion followed by embryo division, or the exchange of a limited number of embryonic cells, or it could be related to the sharing of a placental blood supply – and it is via the placenta that mosaicism goes universal.

Some researchers now believe that we are all micro-mosaic via the placenta, containing quantities of our mother's DNA in addition to that which might now rather more cautiously be called our own, acquired via the placenta. Through the same imperfections in the membranes of the placenta, mothers also contain DNA from their own children. This exists in sufficient quantities to be detected in more than eighty percent of women tested during pregnancy, and in fifty percent of women tested decades later.

Follow the logic, and we all contain DNA not only from our mothers, but also from our maternal grandmothers and beyond; and because women carry DNA from their own children, later siblings will contain DNA from their elder siblings (of either gender), who will have the same mother, but who may or may not have the same father. In the case of girls, the entire mix can be passed on to their own children, the later of whom in birth sequence will also contain the DNA of her earlier children. We are teeming with a whole mixture of DNA.

There may be genuine evolutionary benefit in this internal cellular chaos, benefiting immunity and even encouraging a process of internal natural selection amongst the various genetic lines. Just as intriguing is the possible effect on gender identity and sexual orientation. If we are all XX-XY micro-mosaic, we are all intersex.[40]

The Biblical Eunuch

Within the LGBTI alliance, it is the intersex who finally reveal the queer continuum of gender and sexuality. It is also the intersex who represent the entire alliance by their appearance in scripture, in both the Old Testament and the New.

The biblical eunuch - *cariyc* in the Hebrew Old Testament, *eunouchos* in the Greek New Testament - has been an enigma, a mystery to the respectable western mind, which is bewildered at the thought that such an individual could even exist, much less appear in such conspicuous passages of scripture.

The key text is in Matthew chapter nineteen, where Jesus suggests that many cases of divorce followed by remarriage are morally equivalent to adultery. The disciples respond that if this is the case it may be best not to marry at all.

Jesus's response is worth quoting in full. 'Not everyone can receive this teaching, but only those to whom it is given. For there are eunuchs born from their mother's womb, and there are eunuchs who were made eunuchs by others, and there are eunuchs who have made themselves eunuchs for the sake of the kingdom of heaven. Those who can receive it, receive it.'[41]

The traditional interpretation - made and then almost universally ignored - comes in three parts. Firstly, the disciples are right: it is indeed morally better not to marry at all. Secondly, whilst the first two types of eunuch are to be taken literally, to make yourself a eunuch for the sake of the kingdom of heaven simply means to remain celibate, which is a holier state than marriage. Thirdly, not everyone can 'receive' this teaching, but while those who cannot receive it are indeed morally inferior, they are still acceptable, and are free to marry.[42]

This entire interpretation is strained, and is almost certainly based on a misreading of the text. Jesus's reference to 'this teaching' probably refers not to the ungrateful response of the disciples but to his own immediately preceding teaching about divorce and remarriage. His response to the disciples' negativity can then be read not as anti-marriage but as pro-marriage. 'This teaching about divorce and the sanctity of marriage is indeed a difficult teaching. If you are a eunuch - for any of these reasons - then this teaching isn't for you; but for everyone else: commit to your marriage, and stay with it if you possibly can.' Not only is this a valid interpretation of this particular saying in its context, it is also far more consistent with the rest of scripture on the theme of marriage.

Equally significant is what the saying brings to the LGBTI alliance. It brings a gospel affirmation to at least three categories of people who are not called to marriage, namely those born eunuchs, those made eunuchs by others, and those who have made themselves eunuchs for the sake of the kingdom of heaven.

Of these three categories, only the middle one ('made eunuchs by others') has received significant attention, albeit with a certain embarrassment. The widespread presence of eunuchs in royal courts for thousands of years throughout the eastern empires is acknowledged (*cariyc* is used forty times in the Old Testament in this context), assumed to be an ancient and virtually incomprehensible practice about which little more needs to be said for a contemporary western readership. Those in the first category ('born eunuchs') are assumed to be rare and invisible unfortunates of ancient times. The third category is assumed to refer only to voluntary celibacy, as any other interpretation is too dramatic to contemplate.

This bland interpretation has missed entirely the dramatic significance of this text. What we have in this quotation is a direct gospel affirmation of the complex lives of the intersex and the transgendered, and through them the entire LGBTIQ alliance. There is even a confident cross-cultural and pluralist affirmation.

To begin at the beginning, the phrase 'those born eunuchs' may not be the current politically-correct language - as archaic and unwelcome as the term 'hermaphrodite' - but these are the intersex, here recognised in the words of Jesus himself. Even in the contemporary west, one birth in five hundred is referred for surgery - almost always a form of castration - on being identified as intersex. The number of intersex individuals may have been even higher without the general levels of healthcare and nutrition of the contemporary west. As first on the list, Jesus here welcomes the intersex into the biblical category of *eunouchos*.

Next come those 'made eunuchs by others'. These would be known in Israel at the time as a cultural phenomenon from other places, Israel being the great cultural crossroads at the meeting of four continents. Those defeated in war would be emasculated as a final humiliation. Slaves would be emasculated for their owner's convenience, deliberately limiting their options and aspirations. Criminals would be castrated as punishment - something that still appeals to parts of the western psyche for certain crimes. And the dynasties of countless empires, for thousands of years, from Africa to China, would staff their royal courts with eunuchs, regarded as trustworthy and unthreatening servants around powerful men and their many wives. The phenomenon survived into the twentieth century: the last eunuch of the last emperor of China was Sun Yaoting, born 1902, died 1996. The crude operation was performed by his family in 1911, seeking a way out of poverty, just months before the fall of the Manchu Dynasty. In the event he spent much of his life serving China's traditional religion in various temples staffed largely by fellow eunuchs. All of these Jesus welcomes into the biblical category of *eunouchos.*

In the modern west, the catholic religion not only became the hiding place for the castrati, but effectively encouraged their creation. For more than three hundred years castrati were created in childhood, often once again by poor parents looking for a way out of poverty, that they might sing as adults with unbroken treble voices. Some became famous and wealthy. Countless more spent their lives serving mundane churches as singers or as lay servants of the parish. This phenomenon also survived into the twentieth century. Alessandro Moreschi, the last of the deliberately-created, musically-trained castrati, died in 1922.

Finally there are those who, inexplicably, have 'made themselves eunuchs for the sake of the kingdom of heaven'. The key to this otherwise mysterious concept can be found in the religious nature of the hijra communities of the Indian subcontinent. Hijra communities are modelled on other single-sex religious communities, as found throughout the world and throughout history, with a guru or mother figure, a sisterhood, initiates and novices. They are made up of male individuals who dress as women, but rather than seeking to pass as women, live as hijra, sometimes called the third sex. The transition from novice to hijra is marked by surgical castration, referred to as *nirvan* (rebirth). The one carrying out the operation is called *dai,* which means midwife. By some estimates as many as one in five hundred of the subcontinent's population may be living as hijra, in accordance with a variety of regional variations. The hijra understand themselves as religious communities devoted to the goddess Bahuchara Mata. They speak of having had a vocation or spiritual calling to become her devotees, to become hijra, from early childhood. The sacrifice of the genitals is the mark of devotion by which they are reborn and enter into the blessed state to which they were privileged to be called. In various eras they had not only religious but royal duties: they would have passed through the holy land in groups like other royal eunuchs. With an inner conviction understood in terms of religious devotion, the hijra have 'made themselves eunuchs for the sake of the kingdom of heaven'. It may be one notch away on the infinitely variable scale of queer sexuality, but comparisons with the contemporary western transgender experience are inescapable: here is their ancient precedent, and their biblical affirmation. It is about finding wholeness and personal integrity in responding to an inescapable spiritual calling; both the social transition and the surgery are 'for the sake of the kingdom of heaven'.

The connection between sexual minorities and royalty will not have escaped gay men ('queens') of a certain age: even today the palaces of the House of Windsor are supposed to be a sympathetic cruising ground for a certain kind of gay sexuality. A sense of community was also of great importance to gay men of a certain generation; and the inescapable sense of vocation or calling, present from an early age, is also known to gay people of all ages, male and female. The hijra even provide a link to that other timeless and global sexual minority, the non-marrying phenomenon which is the single-sex religious community, strongly affirmed in the western tradition.

Jesus listed every non-marrying sexual minority that he knew. If he had known more, he would have listed them. He scoops them all up into the biblical category of *eunouchos* – a category deliberately affirmed in both the prophet Isaiah and the Acts of the Apostles. Unsurprisingly the category is first condemned and excluded in the legalistic book of Deuteronomy.[43] This exclusion and condemnation is then deliberately reversed in both Isaiah and the Acts of the Apostles. In an era of conversions and baptisms by the thousand,[44] Acts chapter eight deliberately includes the detailed story of the baptism of an Ethiopian eunuch into the Christian community by Saint Philip.[45] The previous specific exclusion is replaced by explicit inclusion. The affirmation in Isaiah is more positive still. 'Do not let the eunuch say, I am a dry tree, for the Lord says to the eunuchs, Within my house and within my walls I give you a place better than that of sons and daughters'.[46]

Celibacy - breaking the monopoly

The sexual minority which is the non-marrying, single-sex religious community is known in cultures throughout the world and throughout history. The importance of the western tradition's celebration of this sexual minority should not be underestimated, as it breaks the moral monopoly of heterosexual marriage, and does so with absolute confidence. The tradition even celebrates multiple varieties of this sexual minority: male and female; in community or in isolation; with the primary focus on prayer or with the primary focus on good works; instead of marriage or in widowhood; under vows permanent or temporary, or with no vows at all.[47] 'Accepted with a joyous heart, celibacy radiantly proclaims the Reign of God'.[48]

It is accepted that celibacy is not every individual's vocation. For some, chosen celibacy removes a stumbling block to personal growth, while for the majority, sexuality is entirely compatible with their charity and integrity.[49] The largest voluntary membership organisation on earth - the billion-strong Roman Catholic Church - is led exclusively by celibates: its 3,500 bishops and 400,000 priests are all formally professed as celibates,[50] alongside a further 50,000 lay men and 750,000 lay women living as formally professed and recognised celibates in various religious communities,[51] that their devotion - their *eros* - may be exclusively for God and the wider community. It is maintained, nevertheless, that when compared to each other, marriage and celibacy ('celibacy for the sake of the kingdom of heaven') are equal in virtue and equal in glory.[52]

Protestantism has never had such a confident affirmation of the vocation to celibacy; indeed its most significant founding document, the Augsburg Confession of 1530, launches a broadside against it, arguing that marriage is directly commanded by God, condemning the useless, self-righteous vanity of those who presume to hide away from the world rather than engage with it, and granting only the most grudging exception for those who might voluntarily associate together for a time for a particular purpose such as education.[53] Protestantism proper has never recovered: even the catholic-protestant mix which is Anglicanism took three hundred years to resume the recognition of celibacy as a vocation, with the nineteenth century post-reformation re-establishment of religious communities. Heterosexual marriage retains its monopolising grip on the culture of protestantism, despite Saint Paul's confident commendation of celibacy as a positive option,[54] Jesus's assertion that there is no marriage in heaven, where we shall instead be 'like the angels',[55] and of course the example of the unmarried Jesus himself.

Having come to understand marriage and celibacy as distinct vocations for distinct categories of individuals, the catholic tradition should be in a position to recognise additional categories of individuals and their vocations - those categories we have recognised as LGBTIQ, who are symbolically baptised by Saint Philip in the baptism of the Ethiopian eunuch, and to whom, in the words of the prophet Isaiah, God will grant a place better than that of sons and daughters. This process of recognition has even begun: while Anglican archbishops in Africa continue to deny the existence of homosexuality in their own cultures, and protestants in the west seek and fail to cure homosexuals of their affliction and make them straight,[56] the Roman Catholic church recognises homosexuals as a category, and argues in their defence. 'Homosexuality refers to relations between men or between women who experience an exclusive or predominant sexual attraction toward persons of the same sex. It has taken a great variety of forms through the centuries and in different cultures. Its psychological genesis remains largely unexplained. The number of men and women who have deep-seated homosexual tendencies is not negligible. They must be accepted with respect, compassion, and sensitivity. Every sign of unjust discrimination in their regard should be avoided.'[57] The next step is the recognition of their perfectly healthy *eros* as a vocation, then the recognition of the other categories of the LGBTIQ alliance with their distinct vocations, and ultimately the acceptance that healthy *eros* can emerge from its plural and indiscriminate phase in many forms.

Natural Law and Sensus Fidelium

We have established that reason and scripture both argue in favour of these anti-legalistic changes - but even the tradition of the church is its own critic. Three key aspects of the tradition argue in favour of change: *sensus fidelium,* natural law, and the precedent of the Council of Jerusalem.

The theology of *sensus fidelium* - literally 'the mind of the faithful' - is the idea that the honest beliefs and consciences of the faithful at large are themselves a significant theological resource as valid as any other. The consensus of the faithful today is that couples in civil partnerships are likely to have a love and a faithfulness as rich as any marriage, and the consensus is moving on for other members of the LGBTIQ alliance, if only by virtue of the concepts of 'live and let live' and 'judge not that you be not judged'.[58]

The concept of natural law opens theology to the world of science. It declares the natural world around us to be another significant theological resource, as valid as any other; indeed it insists that our entire theology must be compatible with the realities observable around us. People with homosexual *eros* exist in the natural world, living wholesome and even godly lives. The Indian subcontinent has its hijra, and in Thailand (which has never been any nation's colony) the *kathoey* - Thailand's long-established culture of transgendered ladyboys - make up one percent of the male population, in addition to the ten percent who live as Buddhist monks. Natural law would insist that all these realities are taken seriously: that our overall theology must be compatible with them all.[59]

Finally the tradition of the church established at the Council of Jerusalem in Acts chapter fifteen argues in favour of the full inclusion of the LGBTIQ minorities. The council hears that gentile believers have received the gifts of the Holy Spirit in exactly the same way as Jewish believers, despite having been placed under no obligation to commit to the law of Moses, and having no intention of doing so. The council therefore resolves, on the basis of the evidence, that God, by God's own action, has declared commitment to the law of Moses to be unnecessary for the new life in the Spirit. Christian LGBTIQ communities, partners and individuals today demonstrate the gifts of the holy spirit as richly as any other Christian communities, partners and individuals. The tradition of the New Testament and the Council of Jerusalem would determine that God is declaring, by God's own action, that the religious strictures others would place upon them are unnecessary for - indeed a legalistic hindrance to - the new life in the Spirit.

Contraception

In recent decades - since the papal encyclical *Humanae Vitae* in 1968 - artificial contraception has been outlawed by the catholic church. Before joining the chorus of condemnation for this stance, it is worth pausing to consider whether the church might have had at least some justification at the time for its conservative caution. The edict was issued at a time of major social upheaval coinciding with significant advances in the technology and widespread availability of contraception.

Central to understanding the instincts of both the current pope Benedict XVI and his immediate predecessor John Paul II is their experience of the second world war. For John Paul II, his home country of Poland was overrun and occupied by invaders first from the west then from the east, for sixty years from 1939 to 1989, permanently influencing his attitude to politics, war, and the resilience of culture. For Benedict XVI, growing up in catholic Bavaria, the arrival of the alien influence of Nazism and the ensuing chaos regionally, nationally and internationally instilled a permanent suspicion of any other novelty that might lead to chaos.

In 1968, advances in the technology and widespread availability of contraception were a novelty which the church predicted might lead to chaos. Today the church looks at a culture of divorce, promiscuity and sexually transmitted disease and blames not contraception directly but a culture of sexual irresponsibility made possible by contraception. The suggestion that 'condoms increase the spread of AIDS', widely mocked by the media (its source never quite identified but always declared to be catholic), may not be as nonsensical as it appears. It may be false by a particular type of analysis, localised in both time and location, but in the wider context the statement is not nonsensical. It is certainly legitimate to argue the case that rising rates of sexually transmitted infections amongst the young, and rising rates of teenage pregnancy, can be attributed to a culture of sexual irresponsibility, which in turn can be attributed to the novelty of advances in contraception.

Entirely separate arguments apply within responsible relationships like marriage. Nevertheless, even here, it is worth questioning whether it makes sense to poison all our womenfolk with artificial hormones, or place physical barriers between partners, rather than operate in harmony with the natural cycles of fertility, as the church presently recommends. The church's current stance may be overly censorious, but the natural management of fertility without chemicals or physical barriers does have a certain wholesome appeal and is worthy of consideration.

Placing the question of contraception alongside the ideal of total mutual self-giving opens up several new possibilities in the debate. If sex with contraception is less than total mutual self-giving - the catechism itself says as much[60] - perhaps it does not count as real sex for the purposes either of censure outside marriage or consummation within it, shifting the ethical landscape both for sex before marriage and for the question of annulment or divorce. Permanent sterilisation, in contrast to the provisionality of long-term artificial contraception, could then be regarded as an act of self-sacrifice entirely in harmony with the notion of total mutual self-giving. And within marriage, the artificial awkwardness of contraception might itself be regarded as an act of self-giving self-sacrifice for the sake of marital love.

Natural law theology could contribute to the debate

through a thorough and objective scientific investigation of all measurable aspects of wellbeing attributable to the various options. In the mean time, *sensus fidelium* has already made its decision: surveys report between eighty and ninety-six percent of catholic couples of childbearing age making use of either artificial contraception or sterilisation.

The church's misreading of natural law in this area has been to insist that every act of sexual intercourse must be 'open to life' (that is, to reproduction) in order to be morally legitimate. This has conveniently justified historic opposition to both artificial contraception and homosexuality. Unfortunately it contradicts a whole range of other teachings in the catholic and western tradition: that the marriages of those beyond childbearing age, or those otherwise known to be infertile, are entirely valid; that deliberately restricting intercourse to certain weeks of the monthly cycle in order to avoid conception is legitimate; that sexual intercourse may continue after the menopause; and that sexuality (as *eros*) is to be celebrated in its own right, as an end in itself, without reference to reproduction. A marriage is made by total mutual self-giving, not by the intention of reproduction: sexual intimacy is then an entirely proper and sacramentally necessary expression of total mutual self-giving in its own right, regardless of its 'openness to life'.

Promiscuity, Pornography and Prostitution

To push our exploration of sexuality to its logical limits, even the censored miscellany of promiscuity, pornography and prostitution can be seen as morally ambiguous. Pornography in particular has blurred edges. It is not at all clear where art becomes erotica or where erotica becomes pornography; where the celebration of beauty or sensuality – as in the bible's own *Song of Songs* –

veers towards an unbalanced, self-damaging, objectifying obsession: a praiseworthy celebration of beauty and sensuality may be wrongly accused of being necessarily corrupt and corrupting. The popular image of prostitution is more clear cut and fairly brutal, but here also there are blurred edges around the definition, as first dates are increasingly organised through internet contact sites rather than amongst friends, and romances may involve expensive gifts and a long term imbalance of financial potential.[61]

The question of short term serial promiscuity for those who are not in a couple has already been covered, but the question of long-term alternatives to the couple (in addition to singleness and community) remains. The Metropolitan Community Church was founded in 1968 as a gay congregation in Los Angeles. It now has 43,000 members across 300 congregations in 22 countries celebrating the entire LGBT agenda. Its constitution defines the 'Rite of Holy Union / Rite of Holy Matrimony' as 'the spiritual joining of two persons in a manner fitting and proper by a duly authorized clergy'. Repeatedly - most recently in 2006 - the proposal has been put to its general and regional conferences to delete from this definition the word 'two'.[62]

The proposal is worth considering. In a project called Holy Union, there is no immediately logical reason for limiting the number of participants to two. To go to the extreme, if the word 'many' were imagined in place of 'two', the project immediately brings to mind the western and eastern traditions of single-sex religious communities living under vows. The question remains whether a smaller number of individuals - five or four or three - could form a stable union somewhere between these extremes. The Metropolitan Community Church has repeatedly rejected the proposal, coming to the conclusion that such arrangements are too complex and volatile to declare and bless as permanent unions; and it is worth noting that religious communities, in every culture, have tended to maintain a rule of celibacy, and even to discourage 'particular friendships', as the stability of the community depends on the commitment being to the community as a whole, rather than to particular individuals within it.

I suspect that as human beings with finite resources, we are only capable of managing a certain amount of intimacy at any given time. Most of us invest the majority of it in a partner, and spread the rest around amongst relatives, friends, acquaintances, and some sense of the wider human race. Those in religious communities invest it evenly within the community, then evenly beyond. Our physical relating reflects all this, with sexual interaction as the ultimate expression of intimacy and trust between two partners. In theory there may be particular individuals in particular situations who are able to manage that level of intimacy, with long-term stability, amongst three; but even the instinctively liberal Metropolitan Community Church has decided that such a situation is sufficiently unlikely or rare that it has stepped back from ever offering to declare and bless.

Our ultimate standard remains subjective: human love with integrity, contrasted with human disintegration. From the whole realm of human sexuality, only two recommendations make it into the top ten, the ten commandments: do not commit adultery, and do not covet another person's spouse. This is the call to exclusivity that every lover knows instinctively to be right. The demand for exclusivity is not a possessive imposition on a partner's freedom: it is the deal people choose to demand in exchange for their own self-giving. This deal was hopelessly unfashionable amongst free-thinkers from the 1960s to the 1980s, but in the new century is once again so universal that it nowhere needs to be specified: 'two-timing' is once again a shocking betrayal, rather than an exciting social experiment in personal freedom. The call to exclusivity while in a relationship is in perfect harmony with the notion of human wellbeing.

Reproduction

To choose to bring a child into the world is to make a moral choice of phenomenal significance - and it is indeed a choice, despite any politically correct assumption or nuance to the contrary: a choice on the part of both parents, with the exception only of rape. Children do not appear from nowhere, demanding somewhere to be raised, placing parents under an obligation that they somehow have the right to resent. Producing a child requires a series of voluntary acts. The production of a child may not be a leading motivation in some of those acts, but it is a known consequence of them. All the moral obligation in this situation is with the two adults involved. None of it, at this early stage, is with the child.

The church has traditionally taught that marriage is the only appropriate context for childbearing. It makes this demand on behalf of the voiceless child. Every child has two biological parents. The child has the right to demand that they should be there. That may be beyond what the parents can manage in the end, but it should at least have been their intention at the outset: the child has the right at least to that. The moral compass we have established has no place for condemnation - only a desire for healing for all involved - but as a moral ideal, when the welfare and well-being of a child is at stake, the total self-giving of the parents to the project is an entirely reasonable demand, given their choice to bring the child into the world at all. Ideally they should be there not alternately, but simultaneously, and harmoniously, and indefinitely. It sounds a lot like sacramental marriage; indeed for many today, it is not the moving in together or the marrying that represents the moment of mutually understood self-giving and commitment, but the successful conclusion of a mutually planned pregnancy.

The alternative chosen outcome following conception is abortion. To some it is an entirely logical choice whenever a woman happens to be pregnant and does not happen to want a child. To others it is always morally equivalent to murder.

Within our moral framework based on human integrity, artificial intervention to end a pregnancy must always by definition be part of a process of human disintegration, but to isolate the single act as uniquely corrupt is to misunderstand the complexity of that process. By the time a woman is seriously considering an abortion, her disintegration has already begun, and she may well be contemplating how she can survive at all. Nevertheless, the liberal instinct to support abortion is far from morally unambiguous. With the tabloids baying for the right of parents to design their own offspring - perhaps manufacturing a child to serve as a tissue donor for an older sibling - and science hungry for aborted foetal tissue for medical research, it is suddenly reassuring that at least one organisation has stood calmly against the entire process of artificial intervention in conception and pregnancy. The full pro-life agenda opposes war, promotes rights for the disabled, and supports dignity for the dying. Once we are designing children specifically to have their tissue harvested soon after birth, or organising conceptions purely for the harvesting of foetal cells for others, we have moved into dangerous territory in terms of basic human dignity and integrity.

In an ideal world, no woman would ever find herself contemplating abortion. In our imperfect world, it is better if the business is dealt with before twelve weeks rather than after; better still if sex education for the young could significantly reduce the number of young women who end up contemplating abortion; better still if people who have sex could be doing so without betraying anyone else, and could stay together as a couple to love each other and to raise their child. Taking the wider view, it is a strange culture that performs thousands of abortions every day whilst also intervening in highly intrusive and ethically dubious ways to assist conception in those desperate for a child to raise; and yet to aim the moral case against abortion, and the weight of the law, at distressed pregnant women, can be the worst form of hypocritical, self-righteous judgementalism. Moral effort would be better invested addressing the many different social conditions that leave women contemplating such a distressing choice. There may even be a case for revisiting such traditional resolutions as foundling hospitals, infant adoption, and full social care for the unhappily pregnant.[63]

Back to where we began

Some things return to where they began. Ideological attempts at communal parenting and long-term promiscuity, emerging from the sexual liberation and idealism of the 1960s, have largely been rejected. A new generation of the liberated chooses for itself - eventually - the norm of long-term cohabitation in heterosexual pairs. The vast majority eventually seek for that arrangement the social and legal recognition of marriage. It has even become acceptable again for politicians of the liberal left to praise the virtues of the heterosexual marriage as the best environment in which to raise children: the statistics in this regard are consistent on every measurable outcome from future health and income to involvement with the criminal justice system and mental wellbeing. Marriage remains the enriching, fully human celebration of *eros* and foundation of life for the majority, and the secure home for the next generation.

In the first encyclical of Benedict XVI, the western tradition once again celebrates physical touch, sensuality and sexuality as the incarnation and embodiment of its own highest ideal, and names gratuitous indiscriminate *eros* as the foundation of all love. In our analysis we find it to be true to both the tradition and the scriptures to declare a special place within God's house and within God's walls for the LGBTIQ non-marrying *eunouchoi* and their individual vocations of love, and to encourage all in commitment, faithfulness, stability, and mutual self-giving, with an appropriately genderless rendering of the advice from Proverbs to 'cling to the wife of your youth'.[64]

Seven sacraments, One Yahweh Elohim

The seven sacraments together are the western tradition's timeless embodiment of its humanistic, incarnational faith.

Six of the seven operate within the faith community, celebrating the presence of God in water, bread and wine, human hands, anointing oils and words of compassion.[65]

The seventh - *eros* - is greater. It is acknowledged as universal, operating far beyond the boundaries of the church. Its sacramental ministers are not the ministers of the church but everyone that ever loved. It is the embodiment not of any specific teaching of the western tradition but of its highest humanistic ideal: the self-giving love of one person for another. It touches the fundamental essence of what it is to be human and to be fully alive. It embraces and transcends both body and soul. If the mass is the supreme sacrament of the church, it is matched and complemented by *eros*, the sacrament of home, of society, of life itself.

Within and beyond the sacraments, we name as our God not some distant, dangerous idol or metaphor, but the mystery of infinite compassion. We choose to recognise a spark of divinity - a touch of holy spirit - in everyone and everything. From amongst the countless heroes of the human race we choose Jesus of Nazareth as our leading inspiration. We seek to live in society and in community with compassion and with integrity of body and soul.

This is the authentic western spiritual tradition, not least as compiled into the catholic catechism of 1992. It has no wrathful king, no arrogant judgement, no arbitrary law. It is a journey into the mystery of existence itself and a celebration of all that is good, ideal or divine - all that is Yahweh Elohim - with no place for the god the atheist rightly rejects. It is western spirituality without the wrathful king.

Epilogue

In 2005, I toured the country tracking down my theological college contemporaries. We had all been ordained for life in 1991. Fourteen years later, only half were still on the church payroll.

As well as asking about their experience of church, I asked what they still believed. As good liberals, we shared the habit of answering a question with a question. Do you believe in God? It depends what you mean by God. It depends what you mean by believe. It depends what you mean by 'you': my public self, my private self, myself today, myself in general, my intellectual self, my emotional self, my intuitive self.

One question seemed to break reliably through the facade: is there anything there when we die? Faces would drop, and my former colleagues would talk earnestly about the deaths of their own relatives, and the most challenging funerals they had been called upon to lead.

We were told never to cry at funerals. We had to hold it together so that the family didn't have to. Before I reached thirty I had twice buried people exactly my own age: those were as tough as the infant funerals, of which I lost count. I also did two funerals for well-loved members of my own congregation. For one, we gathered for a vigil mass, late in the night, the evening before the cremation. The other we buried in a persistent rainstorm, heavier than we had seen in years. At the wake - in fresh clothes - we recalled his repetition of the bizarre and otherwise untraceable proverb that God smiles on those who are buried in the rain.

My college contemporaries, on and off the church payroll, spoke about all the infant funerals ('There must be something', as though justice demanded it, and demanding it, made it so), and of their own bereavements, of too many strange coincidences, of a conviction that the best must live on.

Of course the best lives on in those who have learned from it, in the practical good that has been done, and in the countless small ways that the world has been made a better place.

There is nothing to fear if that is all there is.

They say your whole life flashes before you in that final moment. Some have experienced it and survived. Perhaps this is the final self-judgement, as we see it all laid out in a moment, without the time either to build our excuses or to distract ourselves from the simple joys. That final moment becomes our eternity. Others speak of an out-of-body experience, of walking towards the light and into a place of contentment. Science speculates that this common experience may be somehow hard-wired in the brain. Whatever its origin, it sounds like a fine way to go.

It does not matter whether there is anything beyond these experiences; indeed the concept of beyond becomes meaningless if this is the end. Paradise may be nothing more and nothing less than peace at the last, and that is fine.

The end is a mystery, but so was the beginning. To the mystery of the beginning we first ascribed the name Existence or Being, and then, with due caution, the name God. The end is the same mystery. We return to that mystery. We return to God, whatever we have imagined that to be: the dust of the ground, or the atmosphere, or the mystery at the heart of existence itself.

From now until then, for today, for every day that we have breath, the western tradition calls us to integrity: to our highest potential, to fullness of life.

A new generation calls itself spiritual but not religious. People choose yoga, reiki and taekwando. Candles, crystals and gems take on new meanings, selling alongside dream catchers and tarot cards. Ancient and distant traditions are scoured for insight, advice and ritual. Feng shui redesigns our homes. Advice columns promote self-affirmation to realise our dreams. Mainstream medicine goes holistic, examining lifestyle issues amongst the causes and cures of stress.

Absent from this vibrant spiritual marketplace is our own western spiritual tradition. I offer it here as a tradition that is not only profoundly spiritual but also reasonable, sensible and coherent for the mind, touching every emotion of the human heart, and tangible in sacrament and incarnation for the human body and for all of life.

The western tradition names love as its God. It chooses to believe that there is a spark of divinity - of holy spirit - in everyone and everything. It names Jesus of Nazareth as its leading inspiration, its icon and its god. It calls us to gather as a diverse human community of mutual enrichment and care, to hear those stories again, and to share the meal of bread and wine. It recognises *eros* as the origin and ideal of all loves. None of this is for the sake of any notional life beyond death: it is for the sake of the best possible life for today.

When nothing else in the creed or the tradition makes sense, there is love, and to this I cling, indeed I name it my God. I choose to believe in the ultimate *abba pater* nature of all else that exists. I look to the cross, to Christ crucified, as the icon of human life perfected and fulfilled: life lived to the full in a world where power corrupts, and corrupted power crucifies life. Compassion, community and *eros* lift us to a higher place. The sacraments sanctify the ordinary. There is no need for the supernatural: the natural world is wonder and beauty enough.

God without God is about having looked right into the unknown, into the void, without fear. It is about having come to terms with - indeed accepted and affirmed - the entire atheist analysis, and started again. It is about rationally choosing this model for the mystery at the heart of our existence, and rationally choosing this way to live. It celebrates love and Yahweh Elohim, trinity and sacrament.

It is tediously simple to list the faults of the catholic church, but in a building not far from you it has staff and a congregation celebrating the authentic western spiritual tradition with a weekly and daily mass, with the reading of the scriptures, the breaking of bread, and the generous and gracious wisdom of the centuries. Going to mass is a good thing to do. It is a profoundly spiritual experience for over a million in Britain, more than twenty million across the US and over a billion worldwide. It is a good thing to do because it is life-enhancing for this life; there is no condemning god to make an external judgement either way. It is good even to join in those ancient poems that others have called creeds, whether or not there is anything out there, beyond the mystery.

How much of the complexity is easy to believe will vary by the day: some days the full image of a personal complex triune God, other days only the brute facts of our existence and the existence of compassion. Belief is not knowledge, but the model to which we adhere.

We reject the god the atheist rightly rejects, then the mystery of our existence leads us on.

Appendix
The Nicene Creed

Minor variations in the contemporary English text of the Nicene Creed appear throughout the world, as each church attempts to render the original in accessible contemporary language suitable for congregational recitation, whilst catching as many of the subtleties and nuances of the original as possible. Despite these variations, the essential theology of *homoousion* and *enanthropesanta* is not in dispute amongst mainstream Trinitarian churches.

The Roman Catholic church has an authoritative Latin translation which inevitably loses nuances in translation from the original Greek - *dominus* lacks the subtlety and deliberate ambiguity of *kurios,* and it is possible to argue over the shades of difference between *homoousion* and *consubstantialem* - but the real bone of contention between east and west is the Roman (western) addition of the Latin world *filioque* ('and the son') to describe the holy spirit as 'proceeding from' both the father and the son, reigniting the subtle argument (suppressed by the adoption of *homoousion*) about the equality or otherwise of the Father and the Son: eastern instincts have the Father more recognisably primary, western instincts have Father, Son and Holy Spirit all equal within the Godhead. The Nicene Creed succeeds in defining the nature of Christ, but does not develop the full richness of the theology of the Trinity as now understood in the west.

A comparison between the original Nicene creed of

AD325 and the revised text of AD381 is instructive in this regard. The original text includes a rejection of specific alternative ideas about the nature of the Christ, but has nothing at all about the Holy Spirit beyond an unembellished statement of believing in it. The text is compatible with Trinitarianism as now understood, but by no means demands it: it is a 'God and Jesus' creed, with the Holy Spirit wholly undefined.

In the later text of AD381, Holy Spirit is defined as *kurios*, which is a major affirmation in itself, and further acclaimed as the giver of life (*zoopoion*) who is to be co-worshipped (*sumproskynoumenon*) and co-glorified (*sundoxazomenon*) with the Father and the Son.

The earlier text was defined by the Council of Nicaea in AD325, hence the title Nicene Creed. The revised version was defined by the Council of Constantinople in AD381, so the full title of the creed presently in universal use is the Nicaeno-Constantinopolitan Creed, although it is everywhere called simply the Nicene Creed.

The creed of AD381 appears below in the original Greek, in literal translation, and in the official Latin text of the Roman Catholic church. The literal translation and the line numbering are the author's own. Finally there is a word-by-word comparison (in English only) with the text of AD325.

Original Greek

01 Pisteuomen eis hena Theon,
02 patera, pantokratora,
03 poieten ouranou kai ges,
04 horaton te panton kai aoraton.

05 Kai eis hena Kyrion Iesoun Christon,
06 ton Hyion tou Theou, ton monogene,
07 ton ek tou Patros gennethenta
08 pro panton ton aionon,

09 phos ek photos,
10 Theon alethinon ek Theou alethinou,
11 gennethenta ou poiethenta,
12 homoousion to Patri,
13 di ou ta panta egeneto.

14 Ton di hemas tous anthropous
15 kai dia ten hemeteran soterian
16 katelthonta ek ton ouranon
17 kai sarkothenta
18 ek Pneumatos Hagion kai Marias tes Parthenou
19 kai enanthropesanta.

20 Staurothenta te hyper hemen epi Pontiou Pilatou,
21 kai pathonta kai taphenta,
22 kai anastanta te trite hemera kata tas graphas,
23 kai anelthonta eis tous ouranous,
24 kai kathezomenon ek dexion tou Patros,
25 kai palin erchomenon meta doxes
26 krinai zontas kai nekrous,
27 ou tes basileias ouk estai telos.

28 Kai eis to Pneuma to Hagion, to kurion, to zoopoion,
29 to ek tou Patros ekporeuomenon,
30 to sun Patri kai Hyio
31 sumproskynoumenon kai sundoxazomenon,
32 to lalesan dia ton propheton.

33 Eis mian, hagian, katholiken kai apostoliken ekklesian.
34 Homologo hen baptisma eis aphesin hamartion.
35 Prosdoko anastasin nekron,
36 kai zoen tou mellontos aionos.

A literal translation

01 We believe in one God,
02 the Father, the sum of all powers,
03 maker of the air-and-sky and the earth,
04 everything visible and invisible.

05 And in one Lord Jesus Christ,
06 the Son of God, the only-begotten,
07 begotten of the Father
08 before all time,
09 [*Latin adds:* God from God,] light from light,
10 true God from true God,
11 begotten not made,
12 of one substance with the Father;
13 through him [ie Jesus] all things came into being.

14 For us human beings
15 and for our salvation
16 he came down from the air-and-sky
17 and became flesh
18 from the Holy Sprit and Mary the Virgin
19 and became human.

20 He was crucified for us under Pontius Pilate,
21 and suffered death and was buried,
22 and rose again the third day as written,
23 and ascended to the air-and-sky,
24 and took his seat on the right hand side of the Father,
25 and is coming again with glory
26 to judge the living and the dead;
27 his Kingdom will have no end.

28 And in the Holy Spirit, the Lord, the giver of life,
29 proceeding from the Father [*Latin adds:* and the son],
30 who with the Father and the Son
31 is co-worshipped and co-glorified,
32 who spoke through the prophets.

33 And one, holy, universal and apostolic church.
34 I declare one baptism for the remission of sins.
35 I look towards the resurrection of the dead,
36 and the life of the future time.

Latin

The official Roman Catholic Latin text. Sections in square brackets do not appear in the Greek text of AD381. The most likely solution to the argument about whether the opening should be 'We believe' or 'I believe' is that both were used from the earliest times in the original Greek, the plural in a corporate declaration (for example from the council defining the creed) and the singular in a personal declaration (for example at a baptism). The Latin text has *credo,* which is singular.

01 Credo in unum Deum,
02 Patrem omnipoténtem,
03 factórem cæli et terræ,
04 visibílium ómnium et invisibílium.

05 Et in unum Dóminum Iesum Christum,
06 Fílium Dei unigénitum.
07 Et ex Patre natum
08 ante ómnia sæcula.
09 [Deum de Deo], lumen de lúmine,
10 Deum verum de Deo vero.
11 Génitum, non factum,
12 consubstantiálem Patri:
13 per quem ómnia facta sunt.

14 Qui propter nos hómines
15 et propter nostram salútem
16 descéndit de cælis
17 et incarnátus est
18 de Spíritu Sancto ex María Vírgine:
19 Et homo factus est.

20 Crucifíxus étiam pro nobis: sub Póntio Piláto,
21 passus, et sepúltus est.
22 Et resurréxit tértia die, secúndum Scriptúras.
23 Et ascéndit in cælum:
24 sedet ad déxteram Patris.

25 Et íterum ventúrus est cum glória
26 judicáre vivos et mórtuos:
27 cujus regni non erit finis.

28 Et in Spíritum Sanctum, Dóminum et vivificántem:
29 qui ex Patre [Filióque] procédit.
30 Qui cum Patre et Fílio
31 simul adorátur et conglorificátur:
32 qui locútus est per Prophétas.

33 Et unam, sanctam, cathólicam et apostólicam
Ecclésiam.
34 Confíteor unum baptísma in remissiónem peccatorum.
35 Et expecto resurrectionem mortuorum.
36 Et vitam ventúri sæculi.

AD325 and AD381 compared

The text below compares the creeds of AD325 and AD381. Sections removed at the revision are placed in [square brackets]. Sections added at the revision are *italicised.* To read the full text of AD325, exclude the italicised sections and include the sections in square brackets.

Comparing the two creeds, the later text has some minor changes in word order, extensions to the biography of Christ, major additions defining the role of the Holy Spirit, and a new final paragraph that takes the creed beyond the nature of the Trinity to the Christian life.

The line numbering is as above for convenience.

01 We believe in one God,
02 the Father, the sum of all powers,
03 maker of *the air-and-sky and the earth,*
04 everything visible and invisible

05 And in one Lord Jesus Christ,
06 the Son of God, the only-begotten,
07 begotten of the Father, [that is, from the being (*ousia*) of the Father]
08 *before all time,*
09 [God from God,] light from light,
10 true God from true God,
11 begotten not made,
12 of one substance with the Father;
13 through him all things came into being, [things of the air-and-sky and things of the earth].

14 For us human beings
15 and for our salvation
16 he came down *from the air-and-sky*
17 and became flesh
18 *from the Holy Sprit and Mary the Virgin*
19 and became human.

20 *He was crucified for us under Pontius Pilate,*
21 and suffered death *and was buried,*
22 and rose again the third day *as written,*
23 and ascended to the air-and-sky,
24 *and took his seat on the right hand side of the Father,*
25 and is coming *again with glory*
26 to judge the living and the dead;
27 *his Kingdom will have no end.*

28 And in the Holy Spirit, *the Lord, the giver of life,*
29 *proceeding from the Father,*
30 *who with the Father and the Son*
31 *is co-worshipped and co-glorified,*
32 *who spoke through the prophets.*

33 *And one, holy, universal and apostolic church.*
34 *I declare one baptism for the remission of sins.*
35 *I look towards the resurrection of the dead,*
36 *and the life of the future time.*

37 [But for those who say 'There was when he was not', and 'Before being born he was not', and 'He came into existence out of nothing', or who pretend the Son of God is a different substance (hypostasis) or being (ousia), or is subject to alteration or change, these the universal and apostolic church rejects.

Footnotes

Notes to Chapter 1: God

The *Catechism of the Catholic Church,* commissioned by Pope John Paul II in 1986 and published in 1992, is an official, authoritative, comprehensive, single-volume compendium of church teaching. Depending on the edition, it runs to approximately 800 pages, containing 2865 items. Its four parts (based on the creed, the seven sacraments, the ten commandments and the Lord's Prayer) are divided into sections, then chapters, then articles, then paragraphs, and finally the 2865 items, consecutively numbered throughout for ease of reference. The full text is available online at http://www.vatican.va/archive/ENG0015/_INDEX.HTM.

The *Compendium of the Catechism of the Catholic Church* is a shorter précis of the full *Catechism,* running to about 200 pages, in a question and answer format. These footnotes refer throughout to the full edition of the *Catechism,* not the *Compendium.*

1 The 1992 *Catechism of the Catholic Church* items 31, 32 and 34. See the note directly above about the 1992 *Catechism of the Catholic Church.*

2 *Catechism* items 31, 33 and 34

3 *Catechism* item 34

Notes to Chapter 1: God (continued)

4 The Bible is divided into the Old Testament, from before the time of Jesus, and the New Testament, which records the life of Jesus and the early church. The most ancient and authoritative texts of the Old Testament are in Hebrew. Of the New Testament, they are in Greek.

5 In Esther 1:1-2, the Persian (Babylonian) king Ahasuerus (Xerxes I, 485-465BC) is said to reign from his winter residence at Susa over one hundred and thirty seven provinces from India to Ethiopia.

6 Deuteronomy 6:4 – Yahweh Elohim [is] one Yahweh. Quoted by Jesus at Mark 12:29.

7 Exodus 3:14 – God said to Moses, I am what I am; tell the children of Israel that this is who has sent you. The name Yahweh is then derived from 'I am what I am'.

8 Jehovah is the same word as Yahweh, but with inauthentically westernised versions of Y/J and w/v, and inaccurately rendered vowels.

9 The part of the bible recording the life of Jesus and the early church.

10 Genesis 1:26-27, part of the creation story: Elohim said, let us make humankind in our image and likeness.

11 Secondary school ages 11 to 16; 'sixth form' ages 16 to 18.

12 This aspect of the work of Thomas Aquinas (1225-1274, canonised 1323) is in Book I of Thomas Aquinas's *Summa Contra Gentiles*, abstracted in Bertrand Russell's *A History of Western Philosophy*. The idea of counting every existing thing in the universe is from the inaugural lecture of Denys Turner as Norris-Hulse Professor of Divinity at the University of Cambridge, reported by Giles Fraser in

Notes to Chapter 1: God (continued)

Church Times, 10 June 2005. The catechism also discusses whether we can speak of God at all. 'Since our knowledge of God is limited, our language about [God] is equally so. We can name God only by taking created things as our starting point, and in accordance with our limited human ways of knowing and thinking. [But] God transcends all created things. We must therefore continually purify our language of everything in it that is limited, imagebound or imperfect, if we are not to confuse our image of God - the inexpressible, the incomprehensible, the invisible, the ungraspable - with our human representations. Our human words always fall short of the mystery of God.' (Extracted from *Catechism* items 39 to 43.) The ten commandments (Exodus 20:2-17 and Deuteronomy 5:6-12) prohibit the use of any idol - any image of a created thing - to replace or represent the ultimate mystery which is God.

13 John 3:8

14 Matthew 6:25-34 - Do not worry about the basics of life, what to eat, or drink, or wear ... and do not worry about tomorrow, for it has cares enough for itself ... Seek first the things of God; all these others shall be yours anyway.

15 Luke 15:11-32

16 The literal meanings and nuances of this unique and necessary (but increasingly archaic) word include any pleasing, charming or attractive trait, the state of being considerate or thoughtful, mercy, clemency or pardon, approval or favour, privilege, reprieve, dispensation, a sense of propriety or decency, and that which affords joy, pleasure or delight. Grace is always freely given, as an act of pure and unmerited goodwill: otherwise it is not grace, not gracious. Similes include adornment, attractiveness, balance, beauty, decency, decorum, dignity, ease, elegance, finesse, gracefulness, poise, refinement, benevolence, charity, clemency, compassion, forbearance, generosity,

Notes to Chapter 1: God (continued)

good will, indulgence, kindness and tenderness. The Greek is *charis*, which by origin is the pleasing or charming appearance of a fertile field or garden. The original Three Graces of Greek mythology were not Faith, Hope and Charity (these come from Saint Paul in 1 Corinthians 13:13) but Brightness, Joyfulness and Bloom. English derivatives include gracious, gratitude, congratulation, gratuitous (literally beyond that which is necessary), gratuity and - as an antonym - disgrace.

17 Hebrews 11:23 - Moses, when he was born, was hidden for three months by his parents (*pateron*, a plural of *pater*). For cross-reference, in the original story of Moses in chapter two of Exodus, the three months' hiding is done by Moses' mother alone ('when she saw that he was a goodly child, she hid him three months') who then conspired with her daughter to hide him again.

18 The whole parable is actually aimed at them: see the preamble at Luke 15:1-3.

19 This is the opening line of the Lord's Prayer in Matthew 6:9.

20 At Matthew 16:2 Jesus introduces a saying about interpreting the signs of the times with the analogy 'When it is evening, you say, the weather will be fair, for the sky (*ouranos*) is red'.

21 The parable at Matthew 13:32 speaks of 'the birds of the air (*ouranou*)' coming to nest in the branches of a tree or shrub which has grown from the smallest of seeds.

22 For Aquinas, the question is already resolved by our mere existence. All existing things need to be sustained in order to continue in existence. Any living thing needs the right conditions to sustain life. Those sustaining conditions are in turn dependent upon their surroundings to remain in existence as they are, and so on. Only God continues without the need for such sustenance: the ongoing existence

Notes to Chapter 1: God (continued)

of anything else is dependent, ultimately, on God, who sustains all things. God is therefore not only our ancient creator, but the daily upholder of creation, and therefore our nourisher, protector and upholder.

23 Matthew 22:34-40, Mark 12:28-31 and Luke 10:25-28

24 1 Corinthians 13:1-3

25 *Theos agape estin*, 1 John 4:16

26 Encyclical letter *Deus Caritas Est* (God is Love), published 25 December 2005 in Latin, a month later in English translation. The English translation is available online at the Vatican website – http://www.vatican.va/holy_father/benedict_xvi/encyclicals/documents/hf_ben-xvi_enc_20051225_deus-caritas-est_en.html

27 At Matthew 16:13-26, Jesus discusses his role with his disciples for the first time. Peter declares 'You are the Christ, the Son of the living God.' Jesus explains, presumably with a whole range of mixed human emotions, that he will suffer death at the hands of the religious authorities in Jerusalem. Peter 'rebukes' Jesus, arguing that this must not happen; Jesus rebukes in reply, declaring Peter, in the heat of the moment, to be a temptation or challenge (*satanas*) and offence (*skandalon*) to him. In the classic translations this comes out as 'Get thou behind me, Satan'. He then explains to them all the true cost of discipleship: take up your cross and follow me, give up your life that you may find it. *Satanas* here means no more and no less than the abstract nouns temptation or challenge.

28 The image of God as light in the darkness recurs throughout scripture, and forms the basis of the opening verses of the Gospel according to Saint John.

Notes to Chapter 1: God (continued)

29 Genesis 1:26-27. The word for 'image' is repeated for emphasis, *tselem tselem*. The word for humankind is *adam*, used five hundred times in the Old Testament as a generic word for humankind or a human being, and only thirty times for an individual called Adam. Here *adam* means humankind without gender, as it refers to the creation of humankind in the image of God explicitly in both male and female forms. The story of a male Adam preceding a female Eve comes separately later: there are two creation stories in Genesis, distinct from each other and incompatible in detail; the first, with the seven days of creation, is Genesis 1:1 – 2:3; the second, with Adam and Eve in the Garden of Eden, is Genesis 2:4-25.

30 Galatians 3:28

31 Romans 3:23

32 In Matthew 25:31-46, Jesus imagines a future judgement where he commends some for providing him with food, drink and clothing when he was in need, and for visiting him when sick or in prison. He condemns others for seeing him equally needy and neglecting him. Both groups express bewilderment, denying ever having seen him in need. He answers to each group in turn, 'Truly, as you did it (did not do it) for one of the least of these, you did it (did not do it) for me.'

33 The Christian community's meal of bread and wine, known as the mass, or the eucharist, or holy communion, echoes words attributed to Jesus himself: 'This is my body which is given for you; do this in remembrance of me' (1 Corinthians 11:23-25).

34 *Catechism* items 836 to 847 describe, very positively, the church's relationship with (in this order and using these terms) 'the catholic faithful, others who believe in Christ, and finally all mankind', being more specifically: 'those who

Notes to Chapter 1: God (continued)

are fully incorporated into the body of the church'; 'the baptised who are honoured by the name of Christian, but do not profess the Catholic faith in its entirety or have not preserved unity or communion under the successor of Peter' (ie the pope); and finally 'non-Christians' defined as 'the Jewish people', 'the Muslims', 'non-Christian religions', and 'those who, through no fault of their own, do not know Christ and his Church'.

35 Romans 8:23

36 Romans 12:1

37 1 Corinthians 6:15

38 1 Corinthians 6:19-20

39 John 1:1-14

40 'Son of God' is used of Jesus throughout the Gospels and the New Testament. For examples of Jesus being affirmed as God see John 20:28 (Thomas says, my Lord and my God), Acts 7:59 (Stephen cries out, Lord Jesus, receive my spirit), Colossians 2:9 (in Christ dwells all the fullness of the Godhead) and finally Paul's letter to the Philippians 2:5-11 (though he was in the form of God, he took the form of a servant...), which many believe to be quoted from a hymn even older than the letter itself, making it possibly the earliest text in the entire New Testament. John 5:18 and John 14:9 suggest that 'Son of God' and 'God' are equivalent in any case, when applied to the human Jesus ('he said that God was his father, making him equal with God'; 'anyone who has seen me has seen the father'): this matches the western Trinitarian formula, which has Father, Son and Holy Spirit all equally God.

41 This is the origin of the otherwise nonsensical phrase at the end of many Anglican collects, which, having been addressed to God, conclude: 'through Jesus Christ your Son

Notes to Chapter 1: God (continued)

our Lord, who is alive and reigns with you, in the unity of the Holy Spirit, one God, now and for ever.'

42 *Head versus Heart* by Michael Hampson (O Books, 2005) Appendix 1 pages 262-267

43 *Global Catholicism* by Bryan Froehle and Mary Gautier (Orbis Books, New York, 2003) puts the global practicing Roman Catholic population in the year 2000 at 1,045,058,100. This is an increase of 139% on the equivalent figure for 1950, and an increase of 292% on 1900. Over the same periods, the total world population rose by only 117% and 273% respectively, so Roman Catholicism grew as a percentage of world population in both periods as well as growing in absolute numbers. There was growth in both periods on all five continents. Tables pages 1 and 5.

44 The analysis at adherents.com suggests 64,000,000 Lutherans and 73,000,000 Anglicans out of a total 466,000,000 protestants. As well as being the most catholic of protestants, Lutherans and Anglicans are the most globally organised. Other supposed denominational groups are more informally organised, and often doggedly congregationalist in principle and in practice. They range from networks with many millions of members to those with as few as a dozen.

45 An overview of church history before, during and after the reformation era, and up to the present day, forms Part II (chapters 3 to 6) of *Last Rites: The End of the Church of England* by Michael Hampson (Granta Books, 2006)

Notes to Chapter 2: Ethics

1 The full story of Eden and the expulsion from Eden runs from Genesis 2:8 to Genesis 3:24. The section 3:14-19 has a different literary form from the rest (in traditional translations it is set out as poetry, unlike the rest, which is prose), and can therefore be identified as a later addition. This is the only section announcing punishments for the transgression, on (in turn) the serpent (which shall henceforth go upon its belly in the dust), the woman (who shall suffer pain in childbirth), and the man (who will have to labour to till the earth in order to eat). None of the punishments is expulsion from the garden, so the story not only works, but makes more sense, with this incongruous later addition removed. The addition might be regarded as one individual's commentary or meditation on, or interpretation of, the original story, also introducing additional material. The verse 3:20 ('The man called his wife Eve, because she was the mother of all the living') is also out of place, a bizarre interjection at this point. The original response to verse 13 ('What is this that you have done' / 'The serpent beguiled me and I ate') is not any part of the section 3:14-20, but the gentle and gracious verse 21: 'And the Lord God made for Adam and his wife garments of skins, and clothed them', followed by removal from the garden.

2 The scriptures record the ascension of Jesus into heaven forty days after the resurrection - Acts 1:3&9.

3 *Alternative Service Book 1980* (ASB) page 245

4 *Catechism* items 1854 and 1855. There is also an intriguing hint in scripture, in the closing verses of the first letter of Saint John (1 John 5:16-17): 'If you see a sin committed that is not mortal, you should ask, and God will give life for those whose sin is not mortal. There is sin which is mortal: I do not say that you should pray for that. All wrongdoing is sin, but there is sin which is not mortal.'

Notes to Chapter 2: Ethics (continued)

5 *Catechism* items 1857 to 1860

6 *Catechism* items 1451 and 1452

7 *Catechism* items 1459 and 1460

8 *Catechism* items 1452 and 1455 to 1458

9 *Catechism* items 1451 to 1453

10 *Catechism* items 1459 and 1460

11 *Catechism* items 1456 and 1457

12 Matthew 16:19 and Matthew 18:18 both include the saying, 'Whatever you bind on earth shall be bound in heaven, and whatever you loose on earth shall be loosed in heaven.' John 20:23 is addressed to all the disciples, and has the more direct text, 'If you forgive the sins of any, they are forgiven; if you retrain the sins of any, they are retained,' – although the meaning is the same.

13 *Catechism* items 1030 and 1031: 'All who die in God's grace and friendship, but still imperfectly purified, are indeed assured of their eternal salvation; but after death they undergo purification, so as to achieve the holiness necessary to enter the joy of heaven. The church gives the name Purgatory to this final purification of the elect, which is entirely different from the punishment of the damned… The tradition of the church, by reference to certain texts of scripture, speaks of a cleansing fire…' Saint Paul's image of the purifying fire, burning away 'wood, hay and stubble' and so purifying 'gold, silver and precious stones' is at 1 Corinthians 3:12-15, concluding: 'if what you built is burned, you suffer loss, but you yourself will be saved, purified by fire.' Paul refers to the image again in 1 Peter 1:7.

Notes to Chapter 2: Ethics (continued)

14 From *Catechism* item 1033: 'To die in mortal sin without repenting and accepting God's merciful love means remaining separated from God for ever by our own free choice'. From *Catechism* item 1037: 'God predestines no one to go to hell; for this, a wilful turning away from God (a mortal sin) is necessary - and persistence in it until the end'.

15 *Catechism* item 1861

16 *Catechism* item 1033

17 Revelation 2:11, 20:6-14 and 21:8

18 *Catechism* item 1861

19 *Catechism* item 1472

20 *Catechism* items 1472, 1473, 1030 and 1031

21 The *Catechism of the Catholic Church*, commissioned by Pope John Paul II in 1986 and published in 1992, is an official authoritative and comprehensive compilation of church teaching, running to approximately 800 pages, assembled and published as part of the church's ongoing response, decade by decade, to the agenda set by the Second Vatican Council (1962-1965) - and the first comprehensive compilation of church teaching in the church's history. Earlier catechisms were booklets of only a few hundred words, designed for basic teaching ('catechesis'), often in question and answer format.

22 Indulgences are not, generally, offered for sale, but are declared as part of a wider celebration in which those seeking them might participate. See *Catechism* items 1471, 1474 and 1479.

23 Limbo, once the theoretical destination of unbaptised infants, is not even mentioned in the 1992 *Catechism* - all part of the affirmation of a confident ultimate universalism.

Notes to Chapter 2: Ethics (continued)

24 The ten commandments appear at Exodus 20:2-17 and Deuteronomy 5:6-12. In Deuteronomy it is Yahweh who speaks the same words: 'I am Yahweh Elohim, you will have no other gods (Elohim) before me'.

25 As a chilling distraction early in the list, it appears that God threatens to punish the third and fourth generation for the sins of the first. The tragedy is that we know this effect to be true without any divine intervention: a damaged life in one generation so often bequeaths damage to the next. The damage is only 'for those that hate': God shows 'steadfast love to thousands of those who love and keep these commandments'. The promise 'that your days may be long upon the land which the Lord God gives you' comes after false religion, rest, and honouring the parents, and before murder, adultery, theft, perjury and covetousness. The commandment requiring a sabbath day's rest includes an obligation to grant rest to 'your son, your daughter, your manservant, your maidservant, your ox, your ass, your cattle, and the foreigner who is within your gates'. In Anglican and most protestant usage, the prohibition on graven images is the second commandment, after 'you will have no other gods before me'. In Roman Catholic and Lutheran usage, the prohibition on graven images is subsumed within the first commandment, and covetousness at the end of the list is broken into two: Exodus advises against the coveting of another's house, wife, manservant, maidservant, ox, ass, or any other thing; Deuteronomy reorders the list to place the wife first, in a clause of her own, and the catholic usage follows this format to make a list of ten in which adultery and its desire become one commandment each within the ten, further honouring the marriage bond, and presaging the words of Jesus declaring an objectifying lust to be as harmful as adultery (Matthew 5:28).

26 The Lord's Prayer in Matthew (Matthew 6:9-13) has 'forgive us our debts, as we also have forgiven our debtors', using

Notes to Chapter 2: Ethics (continued)

the Greek *opheilema* for debt and *opheiletes* for debtor, but Matthew immediately follows this (Matthew 6:14) with 'if you forgive others their trespasses, your heavenly father also will forgive you', using the Greek *paraptoma*, and so giving us the word used for the traditional text of the Lord's Prayer in English (trespasses). Matthew also tells the parable of the two debtors (*opheiletes* – Matthew 18:23-35) concluding that all should forgive the trespasses (*paraptoma*) of others. Mark also has 'forgive, that your heavenly father may forgive you your trespasses (*paraptoma*)' (Mark 11:25-26).

27 The book of Proverbs assumes from its opening verses onwards that wisdom is righteous, and its opposite is foolishness or folly. The theme is repeated throughout the prologue, which runs for the first nine chapters of the book, before the twenty-two chapters of the proverbs themselves.

28 I have written in more detail elsewhere about the seven deadly sins, specifically the way they characterise distinctive aspects or forms of human disintegration or corruption in contrast to human health and flourishing. *Head versus Heart* by Michael Hampson (O Books, 2005).

29 Matthew 22:36-40, Mark 12:28-31 and Luke 10:25-28

30 *Catechism* item 1472

31 John 10:10 – 'I came that they might have life, and life abundant'. Mark 12:30 and Luke 10:27 both specify 'You shall love the Lord your God with all your heart, and soul, and mind, and strength.'

32 There is more about the Church Langley years in *Last Rites: The End of the Church of England* by Michael Hampson, (Granta Books, 2006)

33 *Alternative Service Book 1980* (ASB) alternative option B on page 165

Notes to Chapter 2: Ethics (continued)

34 The only permitted form of absolution in *Alternative Service Book 1980* (ASB), and the standard form in *Common Worship* (the year 2000 replacement for ASB), reads as follows: 'Almighty God, who forgives all who truly repent, have mercy upon *you*, pardon and deliver *you* from all *your* sins, confirm and strengthen *you* in all goodness, and keep *you* in life eternal, through Jesus Christ our Lord.'

35 The controversy leading to this declaration began when Baptist minister Revd Steve Chalke MBE, one of the UK's best-known evangelicals on account of his television work, criticised penal substitutionary atonement in his book *The Lost Message of Jesus*, comparing it to 'cosmic child abuse', and contrasting its model of a violently vengeful God to the teaching of Jesus about loving even our enemies and forgiving one another. In the course of the controversy Steve Chalke prepared a paper, *Redeeming the Cross*, in which he traces the origins of the theory to a single nineteenth century preacher. Many of Steve Chalke's detractors insisted he was throwing away two thousand years of Christian teaching. 'Initially, though not explicitly, rooted in the writings of Anselm of Canterbury (1033-1109), penal substitution was substantially formed by John Calvin's legal mind in the reformation. The model as it is understood and taught today, however, rests largely on the work of the 19th century American scholar Charles Hodge. Almost all Christians across the world today have heard Hodge's theory preached: a righteous God is angry with sinners and demands justice. His wrath can only be appeased through bringing about the violent death of his Son.'

36 Jesus is initially seen teaching in the synagogue ('as was his custom' – Luke 4:16), and at one stage is on good terms with one of the leaders of the synagogue (Mark 5:22-43, Matthew 9:18-26 and Luke 8:40-56), but increasingly finds hostility there. See Matthew 12:9-13, Matthew 13:54-58, Mark 1:21-28, Mark 3:1-5, Mark 6:1-6, Luke 4:16-30, Luke 6:6-10 and John 6:59.

Notes to Chapter 2: Ethics (continued)

37 Luke 4:28-31

38 Jesus teaches in private homes and at the lakeside in Mark 2 (verses 1, 2, 13 and 15), at the lakeside again in chapter 4, in private homes in Matthew 9:10 and Luke 5:29, and so on through his ministry, spending much of his time outdoors or at meals in private homes. The main compilations of the sayings of Jesus in Matthew and Luke are presented as open-air addresses: the Sermon on the Mount in Matthew chapters 5 to 7, and the Sermon on the Plain in Luke 6:20-49. Jesus's visits to the Jerusalem temple in his final week in Jerusalem (known as Holy Week) are deliberately provocative, and become a major factor in his condemnation and execution at the end of that week (Matthew 21 onwards, Mark 11 onwards, Luke 19 onwards).

39 The theme develops throughout the narrative, but some of the most explicit examples are perhaps the direct condemnations seen in Matthew 23:13-31 and Luke 11:37 – 12:1

40 Matthew 21:1-9, Mark 11:1-10, Luke 19:28-38.

41 Matthew 25:31-46. 'Lord, when did we see you hungry and feed you, or thirsty and give you a drink? When did we see you a stranger and welcome you, or naked and clothe you? And when did we see you sick or in prison and visit you? … Truly, as you did it to one of the least of these my brothers, you did it to me.'

42 Mark 1:32-38

Notes to Chapter 3: Bible

1 Over the centuries the Vatican would determine, from time to time, which texts might be read during the liturgy, but never formally defined the limits of what is now understood as The Bible until the Second Vatican Council in the 1960s. There are many documents in existence, from the second century onwards, containing lists similar to those which constitute the canon of scripture today, but none was formally endorsed by the Vatican or any full council of the church. When the sixteenth century protestant reformers – with their new printing presses – decided that the bible was their authority, they first had to determine what constituted the bible. Even the definition given in article six of the Church of England's Thirty-nine Articles of Religion (promulgated in 1562) sounds strangely unfamiliar, with Ezra and Nehemiah named as the first and second books of Esdras, 'four prophets the greater' counting Jeremiah and Lamentations as a single book, and its list of apocryphal fragments, including the Prayer of Manasseh, being unique to the Church of England.

2 Genesis means beginnings; Exodus means exit, being the departure from Egypt; the title Leviticus refers to the priestly cast, the Levites, descendents of Levi, required to keep the priestly code; Numbers is named for the census in its early chapters, but is known elsewhere as the book of Wanderings in the Wilderness; Deuteronomy means Second Law, being the recapitulation of the law given by Moses to the people, forty years on, immediately before entry into the promised land.

3 This history accounts for the fact that the so-called second book of Samuel contains no mention of Samuel, who is dead before it begins.

4 Hebrews 8:13, Romans 7:6

5 Hosea 6:6

Notes to Chapter 3: Bible (continued)

6 Esther 1:1

7 The 39-book Old Testament is also known as The Hebrew Bible or The Protestant Canon. The Roman Catholic church recognises seven additional books, making 46 in total: the additional seven are known only in Greek, not in Hebrew. The seven are four additional books of history (Tobit, Judith, 1 and 2 Maccabees), two additional books of wisdom (Ecclesiasticus and The Wisdom of Solomon), and one additional prophet (Baruch). These form the core of the so-called Old Testament Apocrypha, along with some additions to the books of Esther and Daniel, also known only in Greek editions rather than Hebrew, and recognised by the Roman Catholic church. Oriental churches variously recognise, in addition, Esdras, which is additional material closely related to the books of Ezra and Nehemiah, 3 and 4 Maccabees, and the fragments known as the Prayer of Manasseh and Psalm 151.

8 The use of the plural name Elohim throughout the Old Testament carries echoes of an ambient polytheism, along with the following explicit scripture texts. Genesis 1:26 - Elohim says, Let us make humankind in our image. Genesis 3:22 - Yahweh Elohim says, humankind (singular) has become like one of us (plural). Psalm 82 - Elohim takes his place in the council of the gods, and addresses the other gods, acknowledging but also challenging and judging them. Psalm 95:3 - Yahweh is great, a king amongst the gods. Psalm 97:7 - All gods bow down before Yahweh. Psalm 97:9 - Yahweh is exalted far above all gods. Psalm 135:5 - Yahweh is great, *adoni* (Lord) over the gods. Psalm 138:1 - I will sing and praise thee before the gods.

9 The relevant group is led out of Egypt by a character called Moses, which is an Egyptian name. This is a strange name to choose for a Hebrew national hero, and is probably therefore authentic.

Notes to Chapter 3: Bible (continued)

10 Mesopotamia – contemporary Iraq – is the supposed birthplace of Abraham.

11 The relevant text (what terms to expect when selling your own daughter into slavery) appears immediately after the ten commandments, at Exodus 21:1-11. It is likely that the Ten Commandments are the text that is out of place here: the narrative flows much more naturally with Exodus 20:1-17 removed.

12 Universal male circumcision. The command is given in Genesis 17:11-14, and again in Leviticus 12:1-3. There is also a habit of the genital mutilation of enemies (1 Samuel 18:27, 2 Samuel 3:14).

13 In Genesis chapter 22, Abraham sets off to sacrifice his only son Isaac, supposedly at God's command, but an angel stays his hand, and a ram is sacrificed in Isaac's place. In Exodus 12:29-30, Yahweh kills every firstborn (of human and cattle) in the whole of Egypt; in Exodus 13:1-2, Yahweh claims as his own every firstborn of Israel, explaining in verses 11 to 16 how they are to be either sacrificed or redeemed with an alternative offering. The assertion of this divine right is repeated at Exodus 22:29, Exodus 34:19-20 and Deuteronomy 15:19, is alluded to in Leviticus 27:26, and becomes the subject of a deal that swaps all the firstborn of Israel for all the Levites and all their cattle in the book of Numbers (3:12-13&40-50 & 8:16-18 & 18:15-17).

14 *Catechism* item 390

15 *Catechism* item 289

16 The book of the Acts of the Apostles has the same authorship and/or editorship as Saint Luke's gospel, and presents itself as a continuation of that account, following the life of the apostles and the early church from the end of the gospel accounts through to Saint Paul's arrival in Rome.

Notes to Chapter 3: Bible (continued)

17 A gentile is anyone who is not Jewish. The word need not necessarily sound exclusive or divisive. In Saint Paul, it becomes the great symbol of inclusion: Paul argues confidently and repeatedly that the gentiles are included as equals in God's plans.

18 The first chapter of Romans describes God's wrath at (which can be read as a metaphor for the waste of human potential in) gentile lawlessness. The second chapter attacks the hypocrisy and judgementalism of legalism in similar terms. In the first twenty verses of the third chapter, Paul struggles to describe the benefit, but ultimate insufficiency, of his own Jewish background. The rest of that chapter describes God's answer to all this human need: righteousness (that is, a status no longer deserving wrath, the true fulfilment of human potential) for all believers, by grace, through faith; not through doing good works or keeping any law, so nobody can boast, and available to Jew and Gentile alike. Chapter four uses the Old Testament figure of Abraham as an example of this justification by faith: importantly for Paul, Abraham was judged righteous on account of his faith long before the law was given to Moses. Chapters five to eight describe the nature of the new life in Christ: its assurance of salvation and its reconciliation with God (5:1-11), and its freedom; the metaphor is freedom from sin and death, with Christ as the new Adam, succeeding where the first Adam failed, and undoing the downfall Adam suffered, so that we can belong not to Adam but to Christ (5:12-end); the practical freedom is from the licentious self (chapter six) and the curse of legalism (chapter seven). Chapter eight is an extended celebration of the Christian life that is lived in the spirit, is destined for glory, and makes us children of God. There follow three more chapters of struggling with the question of how all this relates to God's apparent previous special relationship with Israel, and five chapters of practical advice and instruction, and personal news and greetings, sixteen chapters in total.

Notes to Chapter 3: Bible (continued)

19 1 Corinthians 13 – 'I may speak the languages of earth and of the angels, but without love, I am nothing.'

20 For this reason the two letters to Timothy and the letter to Titus, known together as the pastoral letters, are often thought to be later works by another writer using Paul's name or authority. This author is not entirely convinced, as the Greek literary style is very similar, and it seems churlish to assume that there were no early stable communities to contrast with the exuberant chaos of Corinth and Thessalonica.

21 Acts 18:24-28 – A Jew named Apollos from Alexandria, eloquent and a scholar of the scriptures, came to Ephesus and convinced many Jews, proving from the scriptures that Jesus is the Christ.

22 Paul acknowledges Apollos – and the rivalry of loyalties at Corinth – at 1 Corinthians 1:12, 3:4-6&22 and 4:6; he shows his respect for Apollos at 1 Corinthians 3:6 and 16:12.

23 Romans 7:6 – We are discharged from the law, so that we serve not under the old written code, but in the new life of the Spirit. Hebrews 8:13 – In speaking of a new covenant, God treats the first as obsolete, and what is becoming obsolete and growing old is ready to vanish away.

24 Hebrews 1:2-3; also ascended into heaven, Hebrews 4:14, and glorified, Hebrews 2:9.

25 Hebrews 2:14

26 Hebrews 2:17-18

27 Messiah is literally the anointed one: Messiah in Hebrew, Christ in Greek

28 By tradition the writers James and Jude are not the disciples of the same names, but the brothers of Jesus with the same

Notes to Chapter 3: Bible (continued)

names. Jude is the brother of James in Jude 1:1, James is the brother of Jesus in Galatians 1:19, James and Jude are both brothers of Jesus in Matthew 13:55 and Mark 6:3. James the brother of Jesus and Jude is a leader of the early church in Jerusalem in Acts 12:17, Acts 15:12-21, 1 Corinthians 15:7 and Galatians 2:9&12. There is more on these relationships in the section on the holy family in chapter four.

29 The Sermon on the Mount is a compilation of the sayings of Jesus, presented in Matthew's gospel, chapters 5 to 7.

30 Letter of James, chapter 2

31 There are examples at 1 Corinthians 6:9-10, Galatians 5:19-21, and Ephesians 5:5.

32 For examples see Romans 15:26 and 1 Corinthians 16:1.

33 In Acts 15:20 the council nevertheless defines three laws to be followed by the gentiles: a typical church compromise. The first is a prohibition on eating food prepared according to the customs of another religion: Paul subsequently presents this as a suggestion, rather than a law, in his first letter to the Corinthians (chapter eight). The second is a warning against sexual immorality, which can be interpreted in countless different ways, and nobody would want to remove such a warning entirely. The third is an attempt to impose a subset of the Hebrew food laws on the gentiles, which has been cheerfully ignored by gentile Christians everywhere from that day to this, not least on the authority of Peter's own vision recounted in Acts chapters ten and eleven, and Mark's explicit statement in Mark 7:19, 'thus he declared all foods clean'. It is the process and principle of the council, rather than the detail of its final communiqué, that is relevant to the ongoing life of the church: that if believers receive all the gifts of the spirit despite being gentile, or eating Lancashire Black Puddings, or using contraception, or being gay or lesbian or

Notes to Chapter 3: Bible (continued)

transgendered, the whole church must accept that God has blessed them as they are.

34 The Sermon on the Mount is in Matthew chapters 5 to 7. The Sermon on the Plain is in Luke chapter 6, from verse 20 to the end of the chapter. Matthew, Mark and Luke are together known as the synoptic gospels, on account of their similarities, and their comparison is known as the synoptic problem.

35 The message of Jesus has been summarised as 'father, kingdom, forgiveness', being respectively the underlying principle, the model, and the practical outworking. The Lord's Prayer follows this pattern in its three phases. There is more on this model in the first appendix of *Head versus Heart* by the present author (O Books, 2005).

36 John the Baptist at Matthew 3:2, Jesus at Matthew 4:17.

37 Luke uses a similar collection of sayings, declaring that the truly blessed are the poor, the hungry and the weeping, to whom belong the kingdom of God, and ultimately laughter and fulfilment (Luke 6:20-23).

38 Matthew chapter 5, concluding with 'love your enemies' and the perfection of *pater en ouranois* in verses 43 to 48.

39 Matthew chapter six and chapter seven. Fasting is the religious discipline of going without food for a set period of time.

40 Matthew 7:15-20

41 Matthew 7:1-2

42 Matthew 6:19-21&24-34

43 In Matthew 8:18-22, 'Let me first go and bury my father' almost certainly refers to a father who is still alive, but

Notes to Chapter 3: Bible (continued)

elderly, and who therefore represents an indefinite delay on discipleship. In Matthew 12:46-50, Jesus redefines family as something chosen rather than something given - specifically the fellowship of his disciples rather than his own blood relatives - even as his those relatives are at the door asking for him.

44 Healings and miracles are considered in chapter five, on prayer

45 The only chapter from this section (Matthew chapters eight to fourteen) not summarised here is chapter eleven, in which Jesus discusses the role of John the Baptist, and grieves for towns in Galilee that reject his ministry. Chapter eleven also contains three intriguing verses (verses twentyfive to twentyseven) which have the distinctive literary style not of Matthew but of John. It is a mystery how they came to be here, and of course it is a greater mystery to speculate whether or not this literary style accurately reflects one style of authentic teaching by Jesus himself. The section is known as the bolt from the Johannine blue. It also appears at Luke 10:21-22.

46 The woman is a Canaanite in Matthew 15:21-28; Greek and Syrophoenician in the parallel account in Mark 7:24-30.

47 The Pharisees are an influential leading sect within Judaism at the time.

48 The Sadducees, like the Pharisees, are an influential leading sect within Judaism at the time. The Pharisees believed in the universal or widespread resurrection of the dead; the Sadducees did not.

49 Matthew 16:5-12

50 Christ means 'the anointed one' in Greek, equivalent to Messiah in Hebrew.

Notes to Chapter 3: Bible (continued)

51 The intervening verses Matthew 16:17-19 ('...You are the rock on which I build my church ... I give you the keys of the kingdom heaven...') appear only in Matthew's account, so it is fairly safe to assume that Matthew has edited this text in from elsewhere, thinking this a convenient point, although it detracts from the tension of the moment as recorded in the accounts, otherwise virtually identical, in Mark 8:27-30 and Luke 9:18-21. The additional text in Matthew may have the same origin as the similar text at John 20:23, which records a post-resurrection saying.

52 Matthew 16:13-28. *Satanas* (as in 'Get thee behind me *satanas*') means accuser or tempter or challenger. When Jesus tells the disciples about the opposition his ministry now faces, and the inevitable consequences of that opposition, Peter says, 'Lord this must not happen to you'. This is a temptation to Jesus, who replies, brusquely, 'Away from me with your temptations', or, 'Get thee behind me, tempter'. 'You are thinking the human way, not the divine way – and what does it benefit anyone to gain the world, but lose their soul?'

53 The eye of the needle was a narrow gate in the walls of Jerusalem designed to allow access for pedestrians while preventing passage for animals.

54 Nazareth is in the region of Galilee, in the north of the Holy Land; Jerusalem is in Judea, in the south.

55 Zechariah 9:9

56 See Mark 11:11&15, where Jesus sleeps on it between seeing the temple and clearing it of the traders; see also John 2:13-15, where Jesus has time to make a braided whip between seeing the temple and clearing it.

57 Matthew 21:13 quotes Isaiah 56:7 (my house shall be called a house of prayer) and Jeremiah 7:11 (has this house, which is called by my name, become a den of robbers?). The peculiar

Notes to Chapter 3: Bible (continued)

incident with the fig tree (Mathew 21:18-19) that follows has been interpreted in many ways; it suggests a Jesus who is almost too human, spontaneously angry, lashing out where it hopefully does not do too much harm. It was not even the right season for figs. Some speculate that the story began as a parable, became corrupted, and ended up as this peculiar incident: see the parable of the fruitless fig tree, cursed by its owner but spared by the gardener, at Luke 13:6-9.

58 The story deliberately resembles that in Isaiah 5:1-7, where the vineyard represents the people of God and the gifts of God.

59 The scribes would be the legal and constitutional experts supporting the legalistic culture of the Pharisees.

60 The accounts compiled by Mark and Luke have a similar structure, although Matthew's is the most organised, with the teaching material so clearly compiled into The Sermon on the Mount in chapters five to seven, and the different phases of Jesus's ministry clearly differentiated. John's gospel appears to have different sources available, includes long monologues in complex poetic Greek, and reports Jesus's annual visits to Jerusalem. Matthew, Luke and John add their own introductions: a nativity account in Matthew, nativity and infancy accounts in Luke, and the poem of Christ's pre-existence as the eternal Word of God in John. All four gospels report the empty tomb and a series of resurrection appearances. Worthy of mention as a single, additional, clarifying quote about the kingdom of God, from Luke's gospel, is Luke 17:20-21: Being asked by the Pharisees when the kingdom of God was coming, Jesus answered them, 'The kingdom of God is not coming with signs to be observed … for the kingdom of God is in the midst of you (or within you, or amongst you)'.

61 Matthew 15:1-9 and 23:13-36

Notes to Chapter 3: Bible (continued)

62 Matthew 7:21-23

63 Matthew 23:13,15,23

64 Matthew 12:22-45

65 Matthew 16:5-12

66 Jesus washes the disciple's feet – the task of a lowly servant – in Saint John's account of the Last Supper (Jesus's meal with his disciples the night before the crucifixion). John 13:1-11.

67 Much the same applies to the daily mass, which reads through Matthew, Mark and Luke every year in sequence from day to day, with extracts from John in Lent and Eastertide.

68 The order of readings at Sunday Mass is Old Testament, Psalm, New Testament, Gospel. Readings from the Acts of the Apostles replace readings from the Old Testament during Eastertide. There is a separate schedule of readings for the daily mass, where the order is First Reading, Psalm, Gospel: once again the gospels are read in sequence, the full cycle completed each year; the first reading then runs on a two year cycle, following a New Testament book in sequence from day to day for most of the year, with just occasional sections of Old Testament read in daily sequence, and almost as many sections of Old Testament Apocrypha.

69 The present Roman Catholic lectionary (arrangement of readings at the mass) was adopted in 1969 as *Ordo Lectionum Missae*. There was significant interest from mainstream protestant denominations in north America even during its preparation in the mid-1960s, with catholic and protestant scholars meeting together as the North American Consultation on Common Texts (CCT). Many North American churches adopted their own versions of the Roman model during the 1970s, and CCT produced its

Notes to Chapter 3: Bible (continued)

official Common Lectionary, a harmonisation and revision of these modified versions, in 1983. The Revised Common Lectionary (RCL) followed in 1992. Many protestant denominations worldwide have adopted RCL, with either the Roman Catholic or RCL approach to the Old Testament, or the option to use either, or three years with one followed by three years with the other on a six year cycle. Many RCL readings are longer than the equivalent Roman Catholic readings (fewer verses are taken out for brevity) with the presumably unintended consequence that fewer of the readings are actually used (the Church of England insists on only two out of the four). It is nevertheless heralded as a major piece of spontaneous ecumenism that so many churches of diverse backgrounds are using many of the same readings Sunday by Sunday.

70 RSV New Testament First Edition 1946; Old Testament 1952; New Testament Second Edition 1971.

Notes to Chapter 4: Creed

1 The full title of the creed presently in universal use is therefore the Nicaeno-Constantinopolitan Creed of AD381, although it is everywhere called simply the Nicene Creed. The full text is analysed in more detail in the Appendix.

2 The return of Christ is less a grand thesis in the New Testament, and more a constant theme. The clearest gospel statement is at Matthew 24:29-31 (with parallels at Mark 13:24-27 and Luke 21:25-28) – 'The sun and the moon will go dark, and the stars will fall from the sky, and all the powers of the sky will be shaken, then the sign of the Son of Man will appear in the sky, and all the tribes of the earth shall mourn (or possibly be cut off or separate) and they shall see the Son of Man coming in the clouds of the sky with power and great glory, and he shall send his angels with the great sound of a trumpet, and they shall gather together his chosen from the four winds (*anemos*), from one end of the sky to the other'. The longest discussions are in the two letters to the Thessalonians. Elsewhere the return is virtually taken as an assumption, with mentions (amongst others) at Matthew 16:27-28 and 23:39, Mark 8:38 and 14:62, Luke 9:26, 12:40 and 18:8, John 14:18&28-29, Acts 1:11 and 3:20-21, 1 Corinthians 11:26, Philippians 4:5, Colossians 3:4, 1 Timothy 6:14-15, Titus 2:13, Hebrews 9:28, James 5:7-9, 2 Peter 1:16 and 3:8-14, 1 John 2:28 and 3:2, and Revelation 1:7, 3:11, 22:12 and 22:20.

3 Matthew 28:1-6; Mark 16:1-6; Luke 25:1-5; John 20:1-10

4 Matthew 28:9-10; John 20:11-18; the story is summarised in the longer ending of Mark, Mark 16:9-11.

5 Luke 24:13-35

6 Luke 24:36-39

7 John 20:19-23

8 John 20:24-29

Notes to Chapter 4: Creed (continued)

9 John chapter 21

10 Acts 1:3

11 The ascension is described in Luke 3:50-52 and Acts 1:6-11, and summarised in Mark 16:19. In Matthew, Luke, and the shorter ending of Mark, the appearances could be read as being limited to one day only, but John grants a full week plus the Lakeside epilogue. The shorter ending of Mark concludes at Mark 16:8, recording only the appearance of an angel. The longer ending of Mark - generally assumed to be a later epilogue - appears to summarise resurrection appearances detailed in Matthew, Luke and John. The lakeside episode in John chapter 21 appears to be an epilogue, as there is a conclusion to the book immediately preceding at John 20:30-31. Only the Acts of the Apostles specifies forty days of appearances concluding with the ascension. The tidiness of forty days of appearances concluding with an ascension is then undone by Saint Paul, who lists his own later encounter with the risen Jesus, as a blinding light and a voice, as if it belonged to the same category as all the other resurrection appearances, albeit at a later time. Paul even writes of an appearance to five hundred people at one time, not recorded elsewhere. Paul's own experience is described in Acts 9:3-9, Acts 22:6-11 and Acts 26:12-18. In 1 Corinthians 15:3-8 Paul lists resurrection appearances to Peter, then the twelve, then more than five hundred people at once, then James, then 'all of the apostles, and last of all he appeared also to me, as to one untimely born'.

12 The timetable of events adopted by the church includes the ascension on day forty of the resurrection, and the coming of the Holy Spirit in Jerusalem on day fifty, as the city was full once again for the religious festival of Shavuot or Pentecost, fifty days after Passover. This follows the timescale given in the Acts of the Apostles chapters 1 and 2.

Notes to Chapter 4: Creed (continued)

13 The collapse of religious observance over the last century is a phenomenon unique to western europe, by which other continents, including north america, are virtually unaffected. This globally and historically unique phenomenon is discussed by the present author in more detail in *Last Rites: the End of the Church of England* (Granta, 2006). Global adherents of Roman Catholicism now number more than one billion, with approximately half a billion Eastern Orthodox and Oriental Orthodox of various communions, and half a billion protestants of various denominations. The percentage of the world's population that is Roman Catholic has grown steadily throughout the last one hundred years. There are more Christian adherents today than at any time in history, not only as a total figure, but as a percentage of world population as well.

14 Matthew chapters 3 and 4; Mark 1:1-20; Luke 3:1 – 4:15, John 1:19-34

15 John 1:1&14

16 Luke 1:36-56

17 Matthew 1:18-25

18 Luke 1:26-56, Luke 2:1-5

19 John 2:1-11. The most natural explanation would be that Mary raises the matter because this is a wedding she has helped to organise, perhaps for another son; she raises it specifically with Jesus, her eldest son, because he is the male head of household in the absence of any father figure.

20 Matthew 12:46, Mark 3:31, Luke 8:19

21 This is the text at Mark 6:3. The parallel Matthew 13:55-56 reads: 'Is not this the carpenter's son? Is not his mother called Mary?' The carpenter is not named. This may be a accidental corruption of the earlier text from Mark, 'Is not

Notes to Chapter 4: Creed (continued)

this the carpenter, the son of Mary,' rather than a deliberate alteration (most scholars regard the final version of Matthew as a later text than Mark). Luke garbles the whole story, as he uses it for other purposes, with Jesus initially well received, and this entire line reduced to 'Is not this Joseph's son?': Luke's is the only version to name Joseph as the father of Jesus, and the most obviously re-drafted, as it becomes muddled over whether Jesus was well-received, as in the city of Capernaum in Mark 1:21-22 and Luke 4:31-32, or rejected, as in Nazareth in the sections already quoted from Matthew and Mark. The Luke text is Luke 4:16-30. John also has 'son of Joseph' in a similar, also heavily reworked, text at John 6:42.

22 John 19:25

23 The twelve minus Judas Iscariot

24 Acts 1:13-14

25 The infancy narratives include the episode about Jesus at the age of twelve, where Joseph is present (Luke 2:41-51).

26 Four brothers are named, and sisters (plural) are mentioned but not named, at Mark 6:3 and at Matthew 13:55-56.

27 Matthew 1:23 quotes – or rather misquotes through mistranslation – Isaiah 7:14. 'A young woman shall conceive and bear a son, and his name shall be Emmanuel.' Isaiah has *almah,* which is young woman, and can refer to a young married woman. The Hebrew word for virgin is not *almah* but *bethula,* used fifty times in scripture. For the sake of Matthew, some argue that in the seven occurrences of *almah* in scripture, the word never refers to a woman who is unambiguously not a virgin, and that specifically in scripture (as opposed to anywhere else) it may therefore mean virgin. Some argue the exact opposite: that neither *almah* nor *bethula* means virgin, and where that meaning is

Notes to Chapter 4: Creed (continued)

required, it has to be specifically explained (as it often is in scripture).

28 This is Luke's stated purpose - see Luke 1:1-4.

29 Matthew 1:18-25, Matthew 2:13-15, Matthew 2:19-23, Luke chapter 2.

30 The western (catholic) tradition casts Jesus's brothers as cousins. An eastern (orthodox) tradition casts them as half brothers, sons of a previously married, and presumably widowed, Joseph. This makes Joseph an older man marrying a younger woman, increasing the possibility that Mary would become a widow, but it remains a mystery that the gospels should make no mention of such basic facts as Joseph's status as a father, Mary's later widowhood, and the role of Joseph's sons in the infancy narrative events, in particular the trip to Bethlehem for the census and the visit to Jerusalem when Jesus is lost at age twelve (both recorded in Luke chapter 2). In this sense the eastern tradition is less compatible with the text as a whole than the western.

31 The fulfilment of a mistranslated prophecy, and unease with human sexuality.

32 His tortured decision to do this is described in Matthew 1:18-25

33 Luke 1:36-56

34 Luke 1:24; Luke 1:18-22 and Luke 1:57-66

35 Luke 1:36-37

36 Luke 2:1-40

37 The despised tax collectors of the gospel accounts were not like today's efficient collectors of contributions towards valuable and essential democratically mandated public

Notes to Chapter 4: Creed (continued)

services. They were collaborators with the occupying forces of the Roman empire: enemy collaborators.

38 Matthew 1:18&25

39 Luke 1:35

40 Mary and Joseph are jointly the parents (*goneis*) of Jesus when he is presented in the temple forty days after his birth (Luke 2:27), and in the temple incident when Jesus is twelve years old (Luke 2:41).

41 Mark McFall's *Virgin Birth Revisited* quotes examples from Homer, Pindar, Sophocles and Aristophanes of *parthenos* being used of a young woman who is not a virgin.

42 The most common natural examples of parthenogenesis are amongst invertebrates. The best documented case amongst vertebrates is a species of lizard which is entirely female and which reproduces solely by parthenogenesis. Artificial stimulation of unfertilised eggs has produced parthenogenesis in turkeys and rabbits, and the *in vitro* introduction of genetic material from another female has produced parthenogenesis in mice.

43 The Melchizedek analogy is at Hebrews 6:19 - 7:3. The original Melchizedek story is at Genesis 14:18-20. In the Genesis account the priest Melchizedek brings out bread and wine, an intriguing link forward to contemporary Christian priesthood. The first hint of the myth surrounding Melchizedek is in the messianic Psalm 110: 'Thou art a priest for ever, after the order of Melchizedek'.

44 Scott Hahn, *Hail Holy Queen* (Doubleday / Darton, Longman & Todd, 2001)

45 The reference making the comparison explicit is at Mathew 19:28, where Jesus says to the disciples, 'You shall sit upon twelve thrones, judging the twelve tribes of Israel'.

Notes to Chapter 4: Creed (continued)

46 Matthew 20:20, Matthew 27:55-56, Mark 15:40-41, Luke 8:1-3, Luke 23:49&55, Luke 24:10

47 Matthew 27:55, Mark 15:40

48 The four lists appear at Matthew 10:2-4, Mark 3:16-19, Luke 6:13-16 and Acts 1:13.

49 They are identified as sons of John in John 1:42

50 They are identified as sons of Zebedee in Matthew, Mark and Luke

51 John 14:22

52 Matthew 10:2-4, Mark 3:16-19

53 Luke 6:13-16 and Acts 1:13. The 1611 English-language Authorised Version (the King James Bible) uses (in both locations) 'Judas the brother of James'.

54 The townsfolk of Nazareth name these four brothers (adelphoi) of Jesus at Matthew 13:55 and Mark 6:3

55 James is a leader of the early church in Jerusalem in Acts 12:17, Acts 15:12-21, 1 Corinthians 15:7 and Galatians 2:9-12.

56 Paul calls James the brother (*adelphos*) of the Lord in Galatians 1:19.

57 Jude is an important apostle in Acts 15:22-32.

58 The New Testament letter of Jude is attributed in its opening line to Jude the brother (*adelphos*) of James.

59 The traditional case for James the leader of the church in Jerusalem being James the brother (*adelphos*) of Jesus depends on whether Saint Paul means 'the Lord's brother' (*adelphos*) affectionately or literally in Galatians 1:19. Paul is not in a gracious mood towards James when he uses the

Notes to Chapter 4: Creed (continued)

phrase (see the context in the first two chapters of Galatians), and he does not use it anywhere else of anyone else, so the argument is compelling. There is then no scriptural or logical case for rejecting the idea that these brothers are also amongst the twelve disciples as James and Jude 'of James'. Continuity from brotherhood in Nazareth to leadership in the early church makes more sense than ignoring for three years and then raising into leadership two *adelphoi* of Jesus, whilst simultaneously acquiring and then apparently losing two disciples of the same names.

60 John 19:25. The text says 'Mary of Clopas'. It is conjecture to insert 'wife' or 'son'. Clopas could even be a place name.

61 Matthew 27:56. The sons of Zebedee are the brothers James and John, amongst the twelve disciples.

62 Mark 15:40. James, in this verse, is *iakobos mikros,* which is traditionally rendered James the Less. One recognised meaning of *mikros*, alongside the obvious small, brief, few and subordinate, is younger in birth order. If Jesus was Mary's firstborn, any *adelphos* of Jesus would be an *adelphos mikros*, and here he is: James the younger brother. Luke's gospel, at the cross, has only 'the women who had followed him from Galilee' (Luke 23:49).

63 For the burial, see Matthew 27:61 and Mark 15:47. For resurrection morning, see Matthew 28:1, Mark 16:1 and Luke 24:10.

64 Acts 1:14

65 The list of the women at the cross in John 19:25 reads 'his mother, and the sister of his mother, Mary of Clopas, and Mary Magdalene'. This may be a list of four people, or it may be a list of three, with Mary of Clopas being the sister (*adelphe*) of Mary the mother of Jesus. The consequences are no less intriguing if this is a list of four people, as it still adds a sister of Mary the mother of Jesus to the group.

Notes to Chapter 4: Creed (continued)

66 This also makes the scene in Saint John's account less dramatic but more comprehensible, where Jesus, from the cross, asks his own mother and 'the beloved disciple' (Jesus's own cousin John) to become mother and son to each other (John 19:25-27): John's own mother is standing there as well, sister of the mother of Jesus, and the four of them are already a family group of blood relatives; all of this without the occasional speculation that 'the beloved disciple' is not John at all, but Mary Magdalene, who is named as present at the cross in all three accounts, taking on a male alias to become author of the fourth gospel.

67 Matthew 10:3, Mark 3:8, Luke 6:15 and Acts 1:13

68 The story of 'Levi of Alphaeus' in Mark 2:13-17, also appearing in Luke 5:27-32, is identical to the story of Matthew in Matthew 9:9-13. The two are assumed to be the same person.

69 Luke 10:1-20

70 Matthew 12:46-50, Mark 3:31-35 and Luke 8:19-21

71 In Matthew 4:12 and Mark 1:14, Jesus begins his own ministry upon hearing of the arrest of John the Baptist. Jesus's time in the wilderness, immediately after his baptism by John the Baptist and immediately before the beginning of his own ministry, is recorded in Matthew 4:1-11, Mark 1:12-13 and Luke 4:1-13.

72 1 Timothy 1:3-6, Titus 3:8-9

73 1 Corinthians 1:12; also 1 Corinthians 3:4-6, 1 Corinthians 3:22 and 1 Corinthians 4:6

74 Galatians 2:11-12

Notes to Chapter 4: Creed (continued)

75 Dan Brown's novel *The Da Vinci Code* - a work of fiction - describes the church's suppression of the bloodline resulting from the union of Jesus and Mary Magdalene.

76 This suppression is already underway as the gospels are compiled, especially the gospel according to Saint John, which names no brothers of Jesus (compare John 6:42 to Matthew 13:55 and Mark 6:3), gives Simon Peter and Andrew an alternative father (John 1:42), leaves Mary at the cross with no sons to look after her (John 19:26-27), and protests just a little too much that the martyred John the Baptist is absolutely not the messiah (John 1:8&19-41).

77 Mathew 27:57, Mark 15:43, Luke 23:51, John 19:38

Notes to Chapter 5: Prayer

1 Mark 1:21-28 (also at Luke 4:31-37)

2 Mark 1:29-31 (also at Matthew 8:14-15 and Luke 4:38-39)

3 Mark 1:32-38 (also at Luke 4:40-43)

4 Mark 1:40-45 (also at Matthew 8:1-4 and Luke 5:12-16) . Jesus also tells those who are healed not to make him known at (amongst others) Matthew 9:27-31 and Mark 3:11-12.

5 Mark 2:1-12 (also at Matthew 9:1-8 and Luke 5:17-26)

6 Mark 2:15-17 (also at Matthew 9:10-13 and Luke 5:29-32)

7 Mark 2:23-28 (also at Matthew 12:1-8 and Luke 6:1-5)

8 Mark 3:1-6 (also at Matthew 12:9-14 and Luke 6:6-11). Luke has two further stories of deliberately provocative Sabbath healings at Luke 13:10-17 and Luke 14:1-6.

9 Mark 4:35-41 (also at Matthew 8:23-27 and Luke 8:2-25)

10 Mark 5:1-20 (also at Matthew 8:28-34 and Luke 8:26-39)

11 Mark 5:21-43 (also at Matthew 9:18-26 and Luke 8:40-56)

12 Mark 6:34-44 (also at Matthew 14:14-21 and Luke 9:11-17)

13 Exodus 16:2-35

14 Chapter six of Saint John's gospel explicitly links the feeding of the five thousand (John 6:1-14) to the theology of the eucharist, including a reference back to the feeding of the Hebrew people in the wilderness (John 6:31), and a long section of eucharistic theology beginning with 'I am the bread of life' (John 6:48-58).

15 Mark 6:45-52 (also Matthew 14:22-33)

Notes to Chapter 5: Prayer (continued)

16 Mark 7:24-30 (also at Matthew 15:21-28)

17 Mark 7:31-37

18 Mark 8:22-26

19 Mark 8:1-10 (also at Matthew 15:32-29)

20 Mark 8:11-13 (also at both Matthew 12:38-42 and Matthew 16:1-4, and at Luke 11:16&29-32)

21 Mark 9:14-29 (also at Matthew 17:14-21 and Luke 9:37-43)

22 The healing of Bartimaeus is at Mark 10:46-52. The equivalent story is a double healing in Matthew, where it appears in one version at Matthew 9:27-31 and in another version at Matthew 20:29-34. Luke's account is at Luke 18:35-43. The crowds on Palm Sunday hail Jesus as The Son of David in Matthew 21:9 and Mark 11:9-10.

23 Holy week fills the rest of each gospel from Mark 11:1 onwards, Matthew 21:1 onwards and Luke 19:28 onwards. The incident with the fig tree is in Mark 11:12-14&20-24 (also Matthew 21:18-22).

24 The Bartimaeus quotation is at Mark 10:46-52 (also Luke 18:35-43 and Matthew 9:27-31). The woman with the haemorrhage is at Mark 5:25-34 (also Matthew 9:18-26 and Luke 8:40-56). The centurion's servant is at Matthew 8:5-13 and Luke 7:1-10.

25 As well as the woman with the haemorrhage, there are those in Mark 6:56 (and Matthew 14:34-36): 'wherever he went, in villages, cities, or country, they laid the sick in the market places, and besought him that they might touch even the fringe of his garment; and as many as touched it were made well.'

26 Luke 4:16-19

Notes to Chapter 5: Prayer (continued)

27 Matthew 11:2-6 and Luke 7:18-23

28 Luke 7:11-17

29 John 11:20-44

30 1 Kings 17:10-2

31 The temptations of Jesus in the wilderness are described in Matthew 4:1-11 and Luke 4:1-13. Jesus is tempted to build earthly popularity and power by pandering to human selfishness, not least by performing miracles (turning stones into bread, or proving himself invincible). He goes on instead to build a ministry based not on miracles but on preaching simple trust in the goodness of God in the midst of every ordinary life. The torment in the garden of Gethsemane is described in Matthew 26:36-46, Mark 14:32-42 and Luke 22:40-46, where Jesus's prayer is: 'If it be possible, take this cup away from me; yet not as I will, but as you will'.

32 *Catechism* items 2565, 2558 (after St Therese of Lisieux) and 2559 (after Saint John Damascene)

33 'Thy will be done' is in The Lord's Prayer at Matthew 6:9-13 and Luke 11:2-4. Jesus's own 'Thy will, not mine, be done' in the Garden of Gethsemane in the hours before the crucifixion is at Matthew 26:39-44, Mark 14:36-39 and Luke 22:42. 'Thy will be done' is also the theme of the temptations in the wilderness at the beginning of Jesus's earthly ministry, in Matthew 4:1-11 and Luke 4:1-13.

34 This is the occasion when he resolves not to return to the place of his growing popularity, but to move on to other towns, to preach there also. Mark 1.35-38 (also Luke 4:42-43 and Luke 5:15-16).

35 Luke 6:12-13

Notes to Chapter 5: Prayer (continued)

36 Matthew 14:22-23 and Mark 6:45-46, also Luke 5:15-16

37 Luke 9:18

38 Luke 9:28

39 Luke 9:37 suggests this, but may be ambiguous. The parallels, Matthew 17:9 and Mark 9:9, do not specify.

40 Luke 11:1-4

41 The temptations in the wilderness at the beginning of Jesus's earthly ministry are described in Matthew 4:1-11 and Luke 4:1-13. Jesus's prayer 'Thy will, not mine, be done' in the Garden of Gethsemane in the hours before the crucifixion is at Matthew 26:39-44, Mark 14:36-39 and Luke 22:42.

42 Matthew 6:5-7

43 The context is the prohibition of retaliation, and the call to love even our enemies: see Matthew 5:44 in the context of Matthew 5:38-47 and the whole of Matthew chapter five, and Luke 6:28 in the context of Luke 6:27-36.

44 Matthew 24:20 and Mark 13:18. This is in the true spirit of those who gave thanks, after 11 September 2001, that the day was no worse than it had been.

45 Matthew 26:41, Mark14:28 and Luke 22:46

46 Luke 22:32

47 John chapter 17

48 Luke 11:5-13

49 Luke 18:1-18

Notes to Chapter 5: Prayer (continued)

50 The story is at Matthew 21:20-22 and Mark 11:20-24. The saying also appears at Matthew 17:20, where the context is the embarrassment of a failed healing by the disciples which Jesus completes, and at Luke 17:6, where it appears with no context at all.

51 Matthew 6:25-34 and Luke 12:22-31

52 The standard format for these prayers in the mass retains a gentle humility. The person leading the prayers does not presume to address God directly. Instead the text addresses fellow worshippers, in the form 'Let us pray for…'. These invitations to prayer are called bidding prayers. Each bidding is followed by silence, during which those gathered, having been invited to pray, have the opportunity to do so, in silence. The biddings can be extempore or prepared, and conventionally focus in sequence on themes relating to the church throughout the world, the nations of the world, and individuals in need. Traditionally there may be a final bidding to pray 'of your charity' for the repose of the souls of those who have gone before – the recently departed, and those whose anniversaries fall at this time. When the bidding format is used, the only prayers addressed directly to God during the entire mass are those read directly from the official text of the mass, and shared therefore with the entire worldwide church.

53 James 5:14-15

Notes to Chapter 6: Community and Sacrament

1 Hebrews 10:25

2 1 Corinthians 12:12,21,27

3 Acts 2:42. 'The breaking of bread' is shorthand for the sacred meal which is the mass.

4 There are four New Testament accounts of this sequence (taking, giving thanks, breaking, giving): in Matthew 26:26-29, in Mark 14:22-25, in Luke 22:17-23, and from Saint Paul in 1 Corinthians 11:23-25. For the giving thanks, Matthew and Mark have *eulogesas*, which is often translated 'blessed', but which literally means 'speaking good words'; Luke and Paul use *eucharistesas* which is more literally giving thanks for a gift. 'Do this in remembrance of me' appears only in Paul and some versions of Luke; similarly 'eat' is only in Matthew, 'take' is only in Matthew and Mark, 'gave' is only in Matthew, Mark and Luke, 'given/broken for you' is only is Paul ('for you' in some texts, 'broken for you' in others) and some versions of Luke ('given for you'), but 'This is my body' is universal, and the choice, on the part of the church, to do this in remembrance, is entirely valid: eating as an equal with all who would come, including the outcast, was a central characteristic of Jesus's ministry.

5 Matthew and Mark have 'This is my blood of the covenant, which is poured out for many'; Matthew adds 'for the forgiveness of sins'. Paul has 'This cup is the new covenant in my blood'; some versions of Luke have 'This cup, which is poured out for you, is the new covenant in my blood'. Only Paul specifies 'after supper'. Luke has the ceremony with the cup before the ceremony with the bread, and with no words except the mournful 'I shall not drink it again', which also occur in Matthew and Mark; some versions of Luke add the fuller ceremony of wine after the bread as well. Paul repeats 'Do this in remembrance of me'.

Notes to Chapter 6: Community and Sacrament (continued)

6 In many places individual communion wafers – symbolic 'pre-broken' pieces – are used, rather than anything resembling actual broken bread. Most places use at least one large wafer, which is symbolically broken, although if is often then (by an unnecessary and rather divisive tradition) consumed exclusively by the priest or priests present. It is entirely legitimate to use these larger wafers for everyone, so that everyone receives a broken piece. They are also available in wholemeal, making them more like bread and less like card or paper: convenient and dignified like the wafer system, while restoring the symbolism of broken bread.

7 These words of the priest at mass are based on the words of John the Baptist recorded in John 1:29: 'Behold the Lamb of God, who takes away the sins of the world'. The image of the lamb relates to the pattern of Old Testament sacrificial offerings. It identifies Jesus as the one who is pure, and whose life will be characterised by making the ultimate sacrifice for the sake of others. 'Happy are those who are called to his supper' is based on Revelation 19:9, where the Lamb, who was slain and is now risen, is host for a great celebration at the end of time.

8 The people's response here is based on the story of the centurion's servant. Jesus travels towards the centurion's house, where the servant is sick, but the centurion sends word to Jesus: 'Lord, I am not worthy to have you enter under my roof; but only speak the word, and my servant will be healed' (Matthew 8:5-13 and Luke 7:1-10).

9 The human community is not made up exclusively of adults speaking independently for themselves: some come as households, including children. Those children are affirmed as full members of the community in baptism: later confirmation gives them the opportunity to affirm their membership and their commitment for themselves as they come of age. The practice of infant baptism affirms the

Notes to Chapter 6: Community and Sacrament (continued)

community aspect of faith, in contrast to contemporary society's unremitting individualism. Of course the baptism of an infant can still be a mockery of the sacrament if there is no commitment to the community on the part of the adults presenting the child.

10 In the Roman Catholic church, the orders of priests and bishops are currently drawn exclusively from the ranks of celibate men (and, slightly bizarrely, married former anglican priests); the order of deacons includes both married and celibate men, but no women. The concept of infallibility can be spun on the basis that every voluntary-membership organisation claims an internal infallibility: if its authoritative body makes an authoritative declaration within the terms of its remit and according to due process, that declaration stands as authoritative and true, within its context, for those who choose to continue as members; in practice most organisations, including the Roman Catholic church, tolerate a certain amount of internal dissent. Regarding 'other gatherings of the faithful outside its own structures', the Roman Catholic church is actually rather gracious: *Catechism* items 836 to 847 extend the concept of authentic faith and practice by stages from those baptised outside the Roman Catholic church to those of any faith or none. By recognising as valid the baptism of those baptised elsewhere, the Roman Catholic church is effectively defining other churches (on its own terms) as rebellious lay communities, outside its own chosen order and organisation, but nevertheless validly part of the church and of the body of Christ; while this may initially sound arrogant, it also has a certain humility about it, as the church admits that its own structures have failed to embrace the whole of God's work in the world, which continues outside its boundaries regardless.

Notes to Chapter 7: Eros and the Seventh Sacrament

1 1 John 4:16

2 Encyclical letter *Deus Caritas Est* (God is Love), published 25 December 2005 in Latin, a month later in English translation. The English translation is available online at the Vatican website. The encyclical has its own paragraph numbering scheme. These opening quotations are from the opening lines of paragraph 1. http://www.vatican.va/holy_father/benedict_xvi/encyclicals/documents/hf_ben-xvi_enc_20051225_deus-caritas-est_en.html

3 *Deus Caritas Est* paragraph 2

4 *Deus Caritas Est* paragraph 1

5 *Deus Caritas Est* paragraph 5

6 *Deus Caritas Est* paragraph 7

7 *Deus Caritas Est* paragraph 5. *Head versus Heart* by the present author (O Books, 2005) is about the integration of head (for logic and reason), heart (for emotions and dreams) and body (or 'gut' as in 'gut instinct' and 'gut reaction') as the three essential parts of what it is to be fully human. The role of the body is celebrated in the introduction to the gut zone on page 24. 'It is in our human flesh and blood that we live out our lives. It is in the body, the physical human form, that we recognize and meet each other, communicate with one another, and organize all of our human endeavours. It is in our incarnation - our embodiment - that we come to birth and live out the fullness of our lives. Ultimately every meeting of hearts and minds is mediated through our human flesh and blood: our five senses, and our words and deeds.'

8 *Deus Caritas Est* paragraph 6

9 *Deus Caritas Est* paragraphs 9 and 10

Notes to Chapter 7: Eros and the Seventh Sacrament (continued)

10 Matthew 22:34-40, Mark 12:28-31 and Luke 10:25-28

11 The emergence of friendship follows the same pattern, beginning with general public politeness and civility, moving on to shorter- or longer-term acquaintanceship, then friendship, and even companionship.

12 *Deus Caritas Est* paragraph 7

13 *Deus Caritas Est* paragraph 8

14 *Catechism* item 1643

15 *Catechism* item 1644

16 *Catechism* items 1626 and 1627

17 *Catechism* items 1626 and 1628

18 Ten US states still (theoretically) recognise unregistered common law marriages. Various problems arise from the legal ambiguity of the status, however, including the handling of disputed divorces, arguments about whether the common law marriage ever took place, the distribution of the estate of someone who has died as a common law spouse, and the possibility that somebody might claim (even years later, perhaps after the person's death) to be the un-divorced common-law spouse of somebody who subsequently registered a marriage to somebody else. In the ten states, the test of a common law marriage is that the couple (i) agree together that they are married, permanently and to the exclusion of all others, (ii) live together, and (iii) present themselves to others as husband and wife.

19 *Catechism* item 1606

20 *Catechism* item 1649

21 *Catechism* items 1625 to 1629

Notes to Chapter 7: Eros and the Seventh Sacrament (continued)

22 Proverbs 5:18

23 *Catechism* item 1629

24 It may even be worse than bereavement, as it can be even harder to let go.

25 The investment encompasses 'body and instinct, powerful emotion, and aspiration of both the spirit and the will' on the general principle that eros encompasses both body and soul. The list is quoted again from *Catechism* item 1643. It resembles the list of the three centres that make up the human individual in the author's *Head versus Heart* (O Books, 2005), where 'head' stands for logic and reason (here, more profoundly, 'aspiration of both the spirit and the will'), heart stands for emotions and dreams (here 'powerful emotion' and possibly 'aspiration of the spirit'), and the so-called gut zone represents the body, and gut instinct, and gut reaction (here 'body and instinct'); each zone has its own intelligence, its own strengths and weaknesses, its own virtues and temptations, and its own contribution to the fullness of what it is to be human.

26 A suggestion from the UK organisation Relate is that there are three key factors for compatibility. None is essential, but if any of the three is missing it is best to have both of the others. The first of the three is shared culture, which encompasses everything from nation of origin and ethnicity to social class and age. The second is verbal compatibility: that you like to talk about the same things, and tend to agree on them. The third is non-verbal compatibility, otherwise described as the magic connection that transcends all explanation, the love at first sight, the bells ringing in heaven, the sheer delight at each other's presence. Any two of the three will do. This model is compatible with the suggested modes for couple compatibility in the author's *Head versus Heart* (O Books, 2005, pages 154-157), where

Notes to Chapter 7: Eros and the Seventh Sacrament (continued)

verbal compatibility is compatibility in the head zone (the home of language), non-verbal compatibility is compatibility in the gut zone (gut instinct, gut reaction, always present tense), and the matter of shared culture is about the assumptions each partner brings to the relationship about how relationships operate or ought to operate, assumptions acquired from the surrounding culture using the intelligence of the heart zone. Closeness in any two of the three will do, with the one potentially disagreeing zone of the three relegated to lesser significance, hence the most common pattern for couples described in *Head versus Heart*, that of so-called neighbouring pairs.

27 Professor Peter D Gluckman (Liggins Institute and National Research Centre for Growth and Development, University of Auckland, New Zealand) and Professor Mark A Hanson (Centre for Developmental Origins of Health and Disease, University of Southampton, United Kingdom): *Evolution, Development and Timing of Puberty*, Trends in Endocrinology and Metabolism Volume 17 Number 1 January 2006. Full document available online as PDF from sciencedirect.com.

28 The first Romance Academy project was led by Rachel Gardner and Dan Burke at Wealdstone Baptist Church, Harrow, North London. It was recorded and televised on BBC2 in three one-hour documentaries in September 2005 entitled 'No Sex Please, We're Teenagers'. During the final month of the five-month project, two teenage members of the original group led a one-month version of the project for a second group of teenagers, and members of the original group spoke about the project in local schools. It took a year to secure funding for a full time post to take the project forward (the post is held by Rachel Gardner), but five more Academy groups graduated during that time, and by November 2006 nine more were running. Twenty percent of those attending the three Academy leaders' training days

Notes to Chapter 7: Eros and the Seventh Sacrament (continued)

held to date have been from secular charities and statutory bodies, and the government is now adopting 'Leave it till later' as part of its youth sex education and sexual health strategy.

29 There seem to be several major reports to this effect each year. These figures are extracted from the report *Freedom's Orphans: Raising Youth in a Changing World* by Julia Margo, Mike Dixon, Nick Pearce and Howard Reed for the Institute for Public Policy Research, published November 2006 (http://www.ippr.org.uk/shop/publication.asp?id=496), by BBC News (http://news.bbc.co.uk/1/hi/education/6075860.stm). Other findings: over the last fifty years, the average age of first sexual intercourse has fallen from twenty to sixteen; the proportion of young people who are sexually active before the age of sixteen has risen from less than one percent to twentyfive percent over the same period; almost a third of those sexually active 15-year-olds do not use condoms.

30 The concept of an age of consent – below which all intercourse is deemed to be non-consensual – was established in English law in 1275, but the relevant age of majority was not specified: commentators quote it variously as ten or twelve. It was confirmed as ten by law in 1576. In 1875 it was raised from ten to thirteen; in 1885 it was raised from thirteen to sixteen only if the partner was over the age of twentyfour, otherwise it remained at 13 until 1956. The new offence of sexual touching, including between under-16s, is introduced in the Sexual Offences Act 2003: see section 13, section 9, and section 78, online at http://www.opsi.gov.uk/ACTS/acts2003/30042.htm. Ages of consent around Europe include 15 (France, Poland, Denmark, Sweden, Czech Republic, Slovakia, Romania), 14 (Germany, Austria, Portugal, Hungary, Bosnia, Serbia, Bulgaria, Croatia), 13 (Italy, Spain) and 12 (Malta). Some of these countries include a special case for age difference, for

Notes to Chapter 7: Eros and the Seventh Sacrament (continued)

example in Italy the age of consent is 13 between under-16s, but if either partner is over 16, the age of consent is 14. Ages of consent in the US differ by state, but the general trend since 1776 has been upwards, reaching 18 in several states, including California, and is 18 under federal law for anyone crossing a state border.

31 Before the 1998 Crime and Disorder Act, the age of criminal responsibility in England and Wales was effectively fourteen, as the prosecution had to establish that anyone aged between ten and fourteen fully understood the consequences of what they had done. Since that Act, the presumption is that they did fully understand, from the age of ten, unless the defence can establish a special case to the contrary. In the US, the age of criminal responsibility varies by state.

32 *Catechism* item 1643

33 In the *Catechism* article on the sacrament of matrimony (items 1601 to 1666) the word spouse or spouses is used 40 times, while bride and groom, and husband and wife, are used only as follows. Using an image from scripture, bridegroom is used once to refer to Christ, and bride is used once to refer to the church, the bride of Christ (items 1618 and 1621). The phrase 'bride and groom' appears in a quotation at item 1622. Sections 1623 and 1624 refer to the liturgies of the church, where the traditional eastern rite crowns the groom first then the bride, and traditional liturgies of east and west alike pray God's grace and blessing on the new couple, 'especially the bride'. The word 'husband' appears in references to scripture, the first (from the Old Testament) being rejected as pre-Christian, and the second commanding husbands to love their wives as Christ loves the church (items 1610/1614 and 1616/1605). The words husband and wife are used symmetrically in items 1627, 1637, 1649 and 1650, with man and wife used

Notes to Chapter 7: Eros and the Seventh Sacrament (continued)

symmetrically in a quotation at 1645. The words man and woman are used symmetrically in twelve items: 1601, 1602, 1603, 1604, 1605 (which asserts that the apparently asymmetrical spare rib creation story actually makes woman man's equal, being 'flesh of his flesh'), 1606, 1607, 1608, 1614, 1625, 1652 and 1660.

34 Similar legislation has been passed in virtually every country in the EU. Legislative battles concerning single-sex marriage are being fought separately in each of the fifty states of the US.

35 The case is presented in detail – verse by verse, Greek word by Greek word – in Chapter 9, 'Use and Abuse of the Bible', in *Last Rites: The End of the Church of England* by Michael Hampson (Granta, 2006, pages 150-163), and so is not repeated in full here; it is a fair summary, however, to describe the supposed biblical case against homosexuality as depending entirely on the misuse, and the wanton mistranslation, of a handful of obscure biblical texts.

36 Other chromosome sets include X0 (Turner Syndrome, one X only, no Y), XXX (Triple-X syndrome), XXY (Klinefelter Syndrome), XYY Syndrome, XXYY, XXXY, and XXXXY. As many as one in two hundred births may be affected.

37 Human male and female genitalia develop from the same gender-neutral pre-natal organs, for example the penis and the clitoris share a common origin, and the seam down the middle of the scrotum in the male is the line along which the two sides of the pre-natal vulva have fused. This fusing of the two sides in males, starting at the lower end, drives the final urethral opening forwards and upwards, and eventually along the penis/clitoris to its tip, resulting in the seam on the underside of the penis; the testes then descend into the fused vulva which becomes the scrotum. In so-called ambiguous genitalia there will be a penis/clitoris,

Notes to Chapter 7: Eros and the Seventh Sacrament (continued)

which may be defined entirely arbitrarily as either a large clitoris or a small penis, and the urethral opening may be anywhere between the perineum and the tip of the penis.

38 Formal attempts to confirm the gender of female athletes began in 1966 at the European Track and Field Championships in Budapest. Women athletes at that event were required to submit to examination by a panel of gynaecologists. Two leading women athletes from the Soviet block failed to attend the examination. The more dignified blood chromosome test was introduced in time for the 1968 Olympic Games in Mexico. This is the test which, in 1985, found Maria Patino to be an XY individual with AIS. She defied the advice of officials to feign injury and leave quietly. Instead she competed, won, and forced a legal battle that continued for two and a half years, at the end of which she was reinstated by the International Amateur Athletics Federation. Details from http://www.medhelp.org/ais/articles/maria.htm. Gender confirmation is no longer practiced universally, but a gender assessment will still take place if a rival team demands it. The assessment is carried out by a team of doctors including a gynaecologist, an endocrinologist and a psychologist. The confusion over the issue of gender is confirmed in at least one example of an athlete being assessed female in 2005 and male in 2006 (http://news.bbc.co.uk/1/hi/world/south_asia/6188775.stm).

39 The Intersex Society of North America is online at http://www.isna.org. The UK Intersex Association is at http://www.ukia.co.uk. The public awareness posters are online at http://www.hinoran.ch/intersex/plakate.html.

40 Since the artificial in vitro creation of mosaics of two different species of mammal, like a sheep/goat mosaic with patches of woolly skin and patches of hairy skin (a mosaic,

Notes to Chapter 7: Eros and the Seventh Sacrament (continued)

not a cross), science has tended to use the more dramatic word chimera in place of mosaic, even for naturally occurring human mosaics. (The chimera is a creature in Greek mythology with a lion's head, a goat's body and a serpent's tail.) This etymologically unhelpful convention is followed in an otherwise helpful review of the current knowledge in this area, *The Stranger Within* by Claire Ainsworth, New Scientist volume 180 issue 2421 (15 November 2003). Ethically and philosophically more complex are human / non-human mosaics: tissue from human foetal internal organs has been transplanted into a developing mouse embryo, human brain cells have been developed inside mice, and various forms of human / non-human chimera embryos have been used for research and medical purposes. For summaries see Sharon Begley, Wall Street Journal, 6 May 2005, *Chimeras Exist, What If Some Turn Out Too Human*, http://www.post-gazette.com/pg/05126/500265.stm; also Maryann Mott in National Geographic, 25 January 2005, *Animal-Human Hybrids Spark Controversy*, http://news.nationalgeographic.com/news/2005/01/0125_050125_chimeras.html.

41 Matthew 19:12

42 This interpretation of 'eunuch for the sake of the kingdom of heaven' is used in the *Catechism* repeatedly – at items 915, 922, 1579, 1580, 1618, 1619, 1620 and 2233.

43 Deuteronomy 23:1 – He who is wounded in the testicles or whose male member is cut off shall not enter the assembly of the Lord.

44 Acts 2:41

45 Acts 8:27-39

46 Isaiah 56:3-5

Notes to Chapter 7: Eros and the Seventh Sacrament (continued)

47 *Catechism* items 914 to 933

48 *Catechism* item 1579

49 Poverty is given a similar role: wealth is a stumbling block for some, but not for all. Poverty and celibacy together are confusingly called 'the evangelical counsels', evangelical here meaning no more and no less than 'in the gospels', and 'counsel' meaning a piece of advice as distinct from a commandment. The 'counsel' to celibacy is the saying about eunuchs for the sake of the kingdom of heaven, in its context (Matthew 19:1-12); the 'counsel' to poverty is in the story of the rich young ruler immediately following (Matthew 19:16-30, Mark 10:17-31, Luke 18:18-30). The catechism's main discussion of the 'consecrated life', lived under the evangelical counsels, is at items 914 to 933. The explicit statement that the counsels may help some but are not for all is at items 1973 and 1974. 'The aim of the counsels is to remove whatever might hinder the development of charity, even if it is not contrary to charity'; in other words, for some people, in some circumstances, wealth and sexuality can hinder the development of charity, but neither wealth nor sexuality is necessarily of itself contrary to charity. 'God does not want each person to keep all the counsels, but only those appropriate to the diversity of persons, times, opportunities, and strengths, as charity requires.'

50 The only exceptions are a handful of former Anglican priests.

51 All these figures are for the year 2000, in *Global Catholicism*, Bryan Froehle and Mary Gautier, Centre for Applied Research in the Apostolate, Georgetown University, Orbis Books 2003, ISBN 157075375X

52 *Catechism* item 1620

Notes to Chapter 7: Eros and the Seventh Sacrament (continued)

53 The full text of the Augsburg Confession (in English translation) is available online at http://www.ctsfw.edu/etext/boc/ac/. The broadside against celibacy is in article 23.

54 1 Corinthians 7:1-17

55 In the resurrection they neither marry nor are given in marriage, but are like angels in heaven - Matthew 22:30, Mark 12:25, Luke 20:35-36.

56 The cult-like ex-gay movement can be found *inter alia* at exodus-international.org, narth.com, and lovewonout.com. The lies and scandals are exposed *inter alia* at www.anythingbutstraight.com/learn/eghistory.html, truthwinsout.com, and exgaywatch.com.

57 Extracted from *Catechism* items 2357-2359

58 Matthew 7:1

59 Homosexuality has also been observed in more than 1500 non-human species, and is well-documented in 500 of them. (Bruce Bagemihl's *Biological Exuberance: Animal Homosexuality and Natural Diversity* formed the basis of the exhibition *Against Nature?* at Oslo's Natural History Museum, reviewed in *The Times* of 3 January 2007, online at http://www.timesonline.co.uk/article/0,,564-2527347.html.) There is no justification, in the human or non-human world, for the statement in *Catechism* item 2357, without further comment, that homosexual acts are contrary to natural law. If other species are intended to be the model, not only is the assessment of other species in this single matter incorrect, but the majority vote would favour aggressive male dominance and male promiscuity, and other 'natural' alternatives would include the consumption of the male partner by the female during copulation (the praying mantis) and the organisation of society as a bisexual

Notes to Chapter 7: Eros and the Seventh Sacrament (continued)

lesbian matriarchy (the bonobo). Natural law theology does better to focus its investigations on what is natural and wholesome for human beings, with both historic and cross-cultural comparisons showing that there are indeed sexual minorities who will flourish best in specific contexts other than heterosexual marriage: the legitimate use of natural law brings science, not prejudice, to theology.

60 'The innate language that expresses the total reciprocal self-giving of husband and wife is overlaid, through contraception, by an objectively contradictory language, namely, that of not giving oneself totally to the other' – *Catechism* item 2370, quoting John Paul II's *Familiaris Consortio*.

61 In both cases (pornography and prostitution) the ethical issues are multiplied tenfold for heterosexuality compared to homosexuality, as the entire feminist analysis of the imbalance of power between the sexes has to be brought into the equation.

62 www.MCCchurch.org

63 The United Nations quotes a global figure of 45 million abortions per year, or more than 100,000 per day. The figure for the UK is approximately 175,000 per year, or 500 per day. Opposing sides in the abortion debate in the US differ little in their statistics concerning the reasons for abortion: less than 1% occur because of rape or incest, and less than 6% because of potential health problems regarding either the mother or the child. Germany has a scheme across sixty cities whereby newborn infants can be dropped off anonymously at a 'baby hatch' – through the exterior wall of a maternity unit into a waiting incubator. Parents take a card with a contact number and have ten weeks to change their minds. An alarm sounds and a nurse is in attendance within two minutes. Japan has introduced a similar system;

Notes to Chapter 7: Eros and the Seventh Sacrament (continued)

India has one planned. http://www.bbc.co.uk/wiltshire/content/articles/2006/05/10/kate_adie_feature.shtml, http://news.bbc.co.uk/1/hi/world/asia-pacific/6657371.stm, http://news.bbc.co.uk/1/hi/world/south_asia/6373043.stm.

64 Proverbs 5:18

65 Water in baptism, bread and wine in the mass, words of compassion in the sacrament of reconciliation, and human hands and anointing oils in the sacraments of healing, confirmation and ordination.

O books

O is a symbol of the world, of oneness and unity. In different cultures it also means the "eye", symbolizing knowledge and insight, and in Old English it means "place of love or home". O books explores the many paths of understanding which different traditions have developed down the ages, particularly those today that express respect for the planet and all of life. In philosophy, metaphysics and aesthetics O as zero relates to infinity, indivisibility and fate. In Zero Books we are developing a list of provocative shorter titles that cross different specializations and challenge conventional academic or majority opinion.

For more information on the full list of over 300 titles please visit our website
www.O-books.net

Other O-books of interest

Beyond All Reasonable Doubt

DR MICHEAL MEREDITH

Exploring the greatest puzzle of all - whether there is, or is not, a Creative Force that many call God.

CONTENT: Here the author shows why mathematics, quantum theory, cosmology, genetics and other forms of science can neither prove nor disprove the reality of God. They raise further open ended questions.

After careful examination of the evidence, ***Dr Meredith*** concludes that neither 'evolutionary' nor 'sacred' information can ever be reliable enough to be the bedrock from which to start a quest to discover the reality of God. To conduct an experiment on the reality of God one must observe from inside the actual experiment. The only ultimate basis of truth is 'being' itself. He describes different orders of experiential proof using narrative and deduction. One class of experience inextricably points to the human mind having the ability to communicate with the transcendental. In deepening and exploring our own experience we can find a language that does justice to both heart and mind. www.dr-meredith.com

Reviews:

"Here is evidence that requires respectful acknowledgement in considering the case for belief in the existence of God." **John Polkinghorne**, *TLS*

"An overriding feature of the book is the humility and scrupulous care that the author brings to his writing... an invitation to make contact with the transcendent within ourselves so that we may know in a similar way."

The Scientific and Medical Network Review

"Genuinely open, scientifically thorough and often colourfully poetic.

Exuberant clarity, the enrichment will extend way beyond the time spent actually reading it." ***Reform***

[1 903816 13] £8.99

Bringing God Back to Earth

JOHN HUNT

- **Why aren't believers better people than non-believers?**
- **Why are there so many religions?**
- **Why did God wait till a couple of thousand years ago to send his son to Earth?**
- **Is God bigger than any one religion?**
- **How do we reconcile what we believe with what we know?**

CONTENT: Religion is an essential part of our humanity. We all follow some form of religion, in the original meaning of the word. But organised religion establishes definitions, boundaries and hierarchies which the founders would be amazed by. This is perhaps more true of Christianity than most other religions, due to the short life of Jesus, his sudden death, the lack of any contemporary records. His teaching about the kingdom of God is great; it could see us through our time on earth. But his followers watered it down and soon lost it altogether. It became a kingdom in heaven for the few, rather than one here and now for everyone. The Church, or Churches, that resulted became increasingly irrelevant, even a hindrance, to seeing it realised.

Many will always find security and truth in the traditions that developed, and good for them. But for those who can't, for those who have given up on religion or never thought it worth considering, the original teachings are worth another look. If we could recover them and live by them, we could change ourselves and the world for the better. We could bring God back to earth.

Reviews:

This is in the nature of an update and a sequel to ***Daddy, Do You Believe in God.***

Answers all the questions you ever wanted to ask about God and some you never even thought of. **Richard Holloway,** former Primus Episcopus and author of *Doubts and Loves*

Knowledgeable in theology, philosophy, science and history. Time and again it is remarkable how he brings the important issues into relation with one another... thought provoking in almost every sentence, difficult to put down. ***Faith and Freedom***

[1 903816 81 5] £9.99